YOU *CAN*
BUY A HOME

You *Can* Buy a Home

Ruth Rejnis

LONGMEADOW
P R E S S

Author's Note

As you are reading these pages, keep in mind that each real estate experience is unique, and you should always use local professional assistance when it is needed. Remember, too, that change occurs constantly in the real estate marketplace, even though certain principles of good investment remain timeless. No book, therefore, can fully substitute for advice needed in a specific area regarding your own finances from a tax advisor, real estate agent, attorney, or other professional advisor.

After reading this book and considering the advice of your professional counselors, the real estate buying and selling decisions are *yours*, based on your own good judgment. Much success and good fortune!

Contents

PART I
How to Prepare for Househunting with Little Cash in Hand

ONE
You *Can*
Become a Homeowner

The difficult we do immediately. The impossible takes a little longer.

—*Slogan of the U.S. Army Air Forces*

Good words to househunt by!

You may feel that buying a home has become well out of your reach. The real estate market seems to you more and more perplexing, and even hopeless.

In the late 1980s, home prices rose dramatically. It was hard for first-time househunters to buy. The early 1990s has been, to a great extent, recessionary. Housing prices have stabilized, or perhaps even dropped, but in many parts of the country they are still too high for the first-timer. Mortgage interest rates may have fallen to the lowest level they have been in many years, but there is still that hurdle of a high downpayment.

"Where," you wonder, "do *I* come in here? The real estate industry, mortgage lenders, newspaper articles—everyone is saying buy, buy, buy. But they don't know *my* situation. I want to own my own home, but I honestly don't see how I can."

Well, reader, you *can*. You can buy a home even if

- you have saved only $2,000 and do not know where the rest of the money you need will come from;
- you feel certain your income is not high enough to qualify for a mortgage;

3

- you live in a part of the country where housing prices are very high;
- you have had credit problems in the past, and are sure your credit report will work against you when applying for a mortgage;
- you are back on good financial footing now, but you filed for bankruptcy just a couple of years ago; or
- you do not want a condominium, but are sure that is all you can afford.

This book will tell you how you can buy a first home through a solid, perfectly unremarkable series of steps. The suggestions and explanations coming up in the next few hundred pages are not offbeat. They do not require having the nerve of a riverboat gambler to pull them off. They are ordinary. They are being used by thousands of others; you will see how many when you start poking around the real estate marketplace. These folks are different from those who resign themselves to not being able to buy because they, while momentarily feeling the weight of hopelessness, soon pull themselves up by their bootstraps and get to work. Their reward for persistence: the keys to their first home.

The market *does* appear difficult for first-time buyers, and is likely to seem so for the next several years. But I firmly believe that many, many renters could be homeowners today if they approached the househunt with the same organization and determination they would bring to a job search—or even to shopping for a new car! Because real estate is such unfamiliar terrain for the first-timer, however, they see figures and price tags and sink back and say, "I just can't do it."

The biggest hurdle prospective homebuyers have to face today—besides their own lack of confidence—is the downpayment. Many can afford a monthly mortgage payment. Perhaps it is likely to be at, or not uncomfortably higher than, the rent they are paying now. But where to come up with $10,000 or $20,000—or, good grief, even more—for that money down.

Is that your concern? There are many suggestions, in *two* chapters in this book, that will help you find that elusive very large chunk of change.

Another deterrent to homebuying, I have found, is that many renters have tunnel vision on the subject. Perhaps you are one of them. When you think of buying a home, do you imagine an attractive single-family house in a good neighborhood in your present community, perhaps on a quarter-acre lot, maybe even *half* an acre? That narrow view of what constitutes a home may be holding you back from owning.

First home and *starter home* are terms you have probably seen frequently in those real estate articles that have convinced you you cannot buy. But look at those words a little closer: note *first* and *starter.* You are at the beginning of a long journey here. If you are in your twenties you will probably own several homes in your lifetime. Even if you are older, you will, in all likelihood, move three, four, or more times.

What you are looking for this time out is what is known as a foothold on the ownership ladder. Forget the dream house this time around. Maybe that will come two or three homes down the road. First-timers must make a *lot* of compromises. Forget how your parents live. You are not likely to be able to *begin* on that level these days.

Keep your eyes on one objective: buying a solid home that you will be able to sell when you want, probably in the next few years, to move up to the next house or condominium. The second one is likely to be more expensive, or larger, or in a nicer neighborhood. And from that home you will move again, no doubt trading up just a little bit more.

Eventually, when you retire, you will probably trade *down*, to a smaller home. Depending on how far you are from that age now, that first house, the one you scrimped and saved for, will have provided you with a nice little retirement fund.

Buying a home is still a good investment. Although nowadays you should be buying more for a decent place to live and fixed housing costs each month than for the money-making appreciation that occurred in the late 1980s. In the long run—and we are talking decades here—your first home will have become the best investment you made. Think of a good solid stock. Over the years there are recessions and small "crashes," but ultimately, a wisely chosen stock will have grown in value handsomely. You just hold onto it and ride out the temporary bad times.

I bought my first home in the late 1970s. I was in my thirties and never would have dreamed two years earlier that I would purchase a two-family house in a small city in the East and become a landlord. I did not have a grand income, and had to scramble around for even the low downpayment needed then.

But I saw the investment potential in having my own place, and I could see that the town in which I was living was becoming so hot I would soon be priced out of the market there. So I took a deep breath and jumped in.

Twelve years later I sold that house during the high-priced days of the late 1980s. I moved to Florida, bought a smaller home, and invested the money left over from the sale. By no means can I afford to retire, or even take it easy, on my house profits, but I cannot help wondering where I would be now if I had rented for the last twelve years and had not taken that first buying step. And it was a move into such a totally foreign—to me—housing style.

Moral: You're ·vise to want to buy. And to consider

unexpected (to you) ways of doing it. Now open up your thinking to the number of possibilities that exist—in downpayments, in financing packages, and in housing styles. There are many institutions and public agencies out there ready to help you!

Once you become a homeowner—and over time that *will* be an experience filled with frustration and bills and even momentary longing for the carefree days of renting— you have realized the American dream. No matter how small the house or half a house or condominium you buy, you will, in the long run, see positive financial results.

In the short term, of course, your mortgage interest and real estate taxes are deductible from federal returns, so there is a very real value to ownership now. The appreciation of your property might be slow, with some years of low inflation and a general economic malaise, but it will appreciate over the long haul. That market appreciation, and the equity you are also building by paying off a mortgage, are forced savings you almost certainly would not have if you did not own a home.

Just a few points of caution before you explore your options, expand your thinking, and consider the possibilities.

• You should not buy if you do not plan to stay in a home at least three years. All of the costs attached to selling a house, buying the next one, and moving will mean you will take a loss on that first home, no matter what you buy, if you move too quickly. This is particularly true in times when annual housing appreciation is slight, if it exists at all. Buy only if you are ready to put down roots.

• You need to get into the buying mindset, if you are not there now. If you plan to purchase a home, you will have to make some sacrifices. Put off buying the expensive stereo equipment, hold down the credit card purchases, and in general retrench and save. Watching every penny is going to be your new life as a homeowner, anyway. Really!

If you want to be able to buy even faster, or buy a more expensive property, you can become even more serious about saving. Forget the lavish wedding you have planned, and have a smaller one, depositing the extra funds in your "house" account. Planning a week's skiing 2,000 miles from home? Stay closer to home and opt for a long weekend at a resort 100 miles away. See how the money adds up.

• Do not forget the expenses that go along with home-owning. You may be worried about a downpayment and closing costs, but feel you can manage, say, a $900 mortgage payment each month because your rent is $800 now. But you will have to pay real estate taxes, water bills, and perhaps trash collection fees where you move. There will be monthly maintenance costs in a condominium or cooperative. There will be endless trips to the local hardware store. There will be repairs for which you, and not the landlord, will be responsible. Keep all of this in mind.

Have you considered all of the above and feel you still want to, and should, buy? Then read on, prepared to discover that searching for a starter home will become almost a part-time, or second, job. It *is* work: reading, working the numbers, making phone calls, visiting homes for sale, and working the numbers again. But your reward is out there waiting for you—your first home.

Tips to Remember

- Get in the homebuying mindset, which means saving money and generally rearranging your priorities.
- Keep an open mind about downpayment suggestions, financing programs, and housing styles. Don't dismiss *anything* without thinking it through.
- *Owning* a house, not just buying one, can be expensive. Be sure that you can afford such expenses as property taxes, water bills, trash collection fees, and repair costs.

TWO
If You're Single and Want to Buy

There is an irony here that may not have escaped you. It has only been in the last twenty years or so that young single people began to purchase homes. They did not wait until they married. They did not wait until they bought with a "significant other." They did not wait until they turned forty. If they could afford a house or condominium, and it made good financial sense for them to buy, they did, even if they were twenty-six years old.

But in the space of the seemingly few years since then, the price of homes has risen drastically, and so, naturally, have downpayment requirements. Now, single would-be buyers seem to be thrown back to the years before the early 1970s. These days, in many, many instances it takes two incomes to purchase a home. Whereas a single person might be able to carry a mortgage payment, there often remains the giant hurdle of the downpayment—and no second income to toss into the pot.

You *can* buy a home even when you think you can't afford one if you keep your mind open to possibilities and do not discard suggestions and novel concepts out of hand. What you are being asked to consider here is buying half a house—and half can well be better than none, as you will see.

This shared-housing style is solid and well conceived, and it is not just for 25-year-olds. Any strapped renter can enter into one of these buying arrangements at any age, and can enjoy the privacy, freedom, investment potential, and tax advantages of ownership. This is a starter home, remember, not the house of your dreams. Could any of the following situations work for *you*?

Sandy and Don

Both are single and work for nonprofit agencies in a mid-size city. They were in their late twenties a few years ago, when they purchased a three-story row house in a revival neighborhood of their city. They were not involved romantically—they were just work buddies.

Sandy wanted to buy a house. She loved her community, and wanted the privacy of a home over a condominium. But she was not handy and was more than a little frightened at the thought of rattling around in seven, or nine, or however many rooms. She could afford a downpayment and the monthly mortgage payment.

Don could not come up with a downpayment, but he certainly knew his way around a tool box. He had a reasonably good-paying job and could carry a monthly mortgage payment.

The two joined together to buy, with Sandy making the full downpayment and Don repaying her gradually by handling much of the renovation work that was needed. His contribution, then, was in the form of sweat equity.

All of this was spelled out in a contract.

Sandy took the floor-through unit on the top floor, Don the floor just below that. The ground floor, which was half above and half below the ground, and which some might call the basement, was converted into another apartment. They deposited the rent from that unit into a joint checking account to pay whatever renovation bills they chose.

Sandy and Don did consult a lawyer to work out all of

the details of their arrangement. And it does work. It is not even difficult to imagine one of them selling—either to the other or to an agreed-upon outsider—and that new half owner continuing the smooth working relationship. This is a business, after all, with all of the whereas and wherefores nailed down.

Dave and Stuart

Dave and Stuart are computer software salesmen. They work together, and their parents vaguely know one another, living in adjacent towns near Boston. The two young men—both 25 years old—were renters in different apartment complexes in that city. Their rents were high, the two felt, as they are in most urban areas.

"We'd sit around and talk," Dave recalls, "and we figured we'd never get anywhere paying all that rent. We really didn't see any point in joining forces to share one rental apartment. We wanted something more solid, something that represented an investment."

"Also," Dave adds, "we kept noticing how prices for houses and condos were rising, and we thought, 'Let's get in on this. We're never going to get really rich from the business we're in.'"

So they went condominium shopping.

The two purchased a three-bedroom, 2½-bath condo unit in one of Boston's suburbs. The city, they reasoned, was just too expensive for each of them to have all the room he wanted.

Both were able to come up with the $15,000 needed for the downpayment on a $145,000 unit. The mortgage payment and all other expenses were split down the middle, in that both had more or less the same income. Again, everything was in writing. Dave said there was no problem with the buying, aside from a lengthy mortgage approval process because of the ages of the two.

Dave took one bedroom and Stuart the second, with the third set aside as a guest room. After about six months in the unit, the two had a long discussion and decided they could not only save by owning, but make some money. They elected to take in a roommate, Jim, who now occupies the third bedroom. Jim's rent, $550 a month, goes toward the monthly mortgage payment, cutting down nicely the amount Dave and Stuart have to pay.

Michael and Edie

Michael came to Los Angeles, having been transferred from Indiana by the corporation that employed him as a salesman. California home prices stunned him, and although he had a reasonably good income, he felt purchasing a home was beyond him.

Perhaps he just did not want to spend as much as it would take to buy in California. He traveled a good deal and would not spend that much time at home, anyway. Still, the tax advantages of ownership appealed to him. "I know that owning is the only way to go," he said. "Even though you could buy four houses, maybe five, in Indiana for the price of one in California."

Edie was a businesswoman Michael had met casually. "We had had lunch once after a conference," he recalled. "She seemed levelheaded and we got to talking about the high cost of real estate here, and one thing led to another." In this case the "one thing" brought them to the decision to buy together. They also realized their travel schedules would allow each of them considerable time alone if they chose to share a home. So they did, splitting the down-payment, mortgage, and maintenance costs.

And that's pretty much where the story ends. They sold the house after two years, and split a $21,000 profit. That was a very good return for holding a home such a little time. Michael said there were a few times they were in the house together, of course, but essentially they were housesharers passing in the night.

"We were both really watching the California real estate market at the time," Michael points out. "We knew this was not a living situation that would last very long, but we wanted to stay in to make as much money as we could before moving on. And California prices had been rising then in the double digits every year."

To Edie and Michael this was a business deal pretty much like a contract to buy office computers or an arrangement to purchase a boat from a friend. Well thought out and executed. No drama.

There are single parents who join forces and buy together. Brothers and sisters buy and share houses. College roommates or fraternity brothers take the plunge and sign for mortgages.

Each of these homeowners has been imaginative enough to see beyond the strictly traditional and say why not to carving out his or her own interpretation of home-owning. Each has been clever enough to see that owning *half* a house is still better, financially, than renting. And that half a house can one day turn into their ownership of the entire seven or nine rooms of the next place—and the one after that. Stretch your thinking and this might work for you, too. Here are some additional points to consider.

• In the early and mid-1980s there was a housing style known as mingles housing that a few developers constructed. These were houses built specifically for sharing. There was a common living/dining/kitchen area, and then separate bedrooms and baths at each end of the dwelling. Mingles housing has not exactly grown like Topsy— probably because of the overall construction slowdown in the early 1990s—but if you do find some of these homes in your area, it might pay you to do a little investigating. Call your local builders' association to see if there is a complex near you.

• Put it in writing is the cardinal rule for sharing ownership of a house. Have a lawyer draw up an agreement for the two (or three) of you, covering every aspect of your buying, maintaining, and selling the house.

• What style of ownership will you choose? Chapter 3 discusses your options.

• Do not buy together without knowing fully the financial situation of your prospective house sharer. These arrangements work better if both have pretty much similar incomes and assets. You do not want to end up toting most of the financial load because your sharer lost his minimum-wage job and your income as a comptroller is now expected to carry the house.

If you want to call yourself an owner and not a renter, this is a starter home style that could work beautifully for you. Agree?

Tips to Remember

- Keep an open mind about buying a home with someone else. It can be a very affordable solution, both to high housing prices and houses that are too large for one person.
- Get everything in writing, from how ownership is split, to resale procedures, to how responsibility for maintenance and repairs will be divided—and every detail in between.
- Buy only with someone whose income is relatively close to yours, and whose values and tastes are at least somewhat similar. That is more important than the potential for becoming good friends with your housemate.

THREE
Buying a Home with Someone Else or Several Others

Owning a house, as you already know, is an enormous responsibility. The key word here is *owning*. The names on the deed to a property are accountable for that piece of real estate—to the mortgage holder, to the insurance company, to the local tax office and utilities, and, to some degree, even to their neighbors, for keeping up the appearance of the place. Despite that burden, the house *is* an asset, an important part of one's estate, which is passed on to whomever one designates in a will.

When there is more than one owner involved, even if the two owners are married to each other, there can be questions about inheritance and tax consequences of the ownership style they have chosen.

This is the stage at which everyone involved in a joint purchase should be deciding *how* they want to buy, so that any problems that surface can be worked out.

When co-owners are not married, the issues become more complex, such as who will maintain the property, what happens when one party wants to sell, and who will inherit a co-owner's share upon his or her death.

Let's start with the simplest buying style for two or more people.

Married Couples

"Well naturally we're buying together," you say. "We'll own the house equally." Of course, what could be simpler? That way, when one dies, the property automatically passes to the other, free of federal estate taxes. That ownership style is known as joint tenants with rights of survivorship.

But just a minute. While that is the most common way for a husband and wife to own, it might not be the best choice. By holding a property jointly, couples raise the likelihood that the Internal Revenue Service could take a bigger share of their wealth than necessary. Also, in some marriages, buyers might want to leave their share of the house to their children from an earlier union.

You have other alternatives to the joint tenants buying style, and you might want to explore them. Choosing "tenants in common," for example, permits each spouse to own half of an asset. Your spouse will inherit your half only if you say so in your will.

Some forms of ownership other than joint tenants can be used even if you both reside in one of the nation's several community property states, where assets acquired during a marriage are usually owned jointly.

Before doing anything about ownership, while you are still at this early househunting stage, consult your accountant and/or estate lawyer. You *do* have an estate, even if you do not own a home. You have furnishings, perhaps a car, jewelry, computer equipment—which all add up to an "estate."

Living-Together Couples

Couples who plan to purchase a home together need to work out every detail of that purchase, which in their case calls for a contract as well as deciding ownership style. The legal system has had its hands full here of late. Cohabitation is still illegal in a few states, including Arizona, Idaho, Mississippi, North Carolina, and Virginia, although those particular laws are rarely enforced.

However, there is little uniformity among the other states regarding the legal status of the millions of couples who "live together," and *that* is a rapidly changing legal arena. Single people may want to pass the property they co-own on to each other, or they may want to will their share to a family member they designate. If you are in this buying position you can choose from among the earlier-mentioned purchasing styles.

Unofficial relationships such as living together are governed by contract law, and when problems arise they might be decided by a jury in civil court rather than by a family-court judge. However, unmarried partners do *not* have the same rights as spouses to share property, among other interchangeable benefits.

To save yourself the expense and pain of taking disputes to court, you will want a strongly written contract covering the questions of ownership, and you will want to keep careful records of all major expenditures and purchases you make while you are together. Yes, this is unromantic—and it may seem petty—but when love flies out the window it is amazing how important money, assets, and estates become.

Imagine that you have bought a condo with a friend and you have each willed your share of the unit to your own parents. Sadly, your friend is killed in an automobile accident and her share is inherited by her father. You now co-own a home with a 60-year-old man you have never met, who lives 1,400 miles away. Are you expected to buy him out? Can he afford his share of the mortgage payment? An agreement drawn up between you and your friend could help you spell out all of the possibilities.

Or imagine that you and your friend have the ultimate fight after months of smaller arguments. It is over between you. You move out and expect not to see her or the house again. But wait. Your name is on the mortgage. You cannot abandon that property and your mortgage responsibility.

There is no law requiring unmarried couples to have a written agreement when they enter into homeownership, but it is the wise step to take. The written contract is not necessarily a prenuptial agreement. It is simply a paper that can cover any number of areas of your life. Since we are talking about homebuying here, however, we will confine ourselves to those related issues.

First, a contract should be in writing. Courts refuse to "assume" partners' understandings by their words or actions. The agreement can be worked out just between partners or with the help of a lawyer. The contract will cover how the home is owned, what will happen in the event the couple separates, and whether the house will be sold then or at any other specified time and how the proceeds will be split. There will be clauses covering any decision about the termination of the agreement, such as on the death of one partner, marriage to each other or to someone else, or just a mutual agreement in writing about termination. A contract can contain as many stipulations as you both choose, about any aspect of owning and maintaining the house.

Are such contracts enforceable? Well, they can be challenged, like any other contract, but a well-written agreement *can* protect partners.

Buying with Friends,
Cousins, Co-Workers,
Fraternity Brothers, and So On

Here you will probably want to purchase as tenants in common, although you might also consider forming a partnership. Your accountant can advise you, particularly if there are more than two of you who want to co-own the home.

A potential problem with one house sharer wanting to sell while the others do not can occur if the lender declares the mortgage must be paid in full when there is a change in owners. This is known as a "due on sale" clause in a loan, and you will want to take this into consideration as you mortgage shop.

Finally, you might also specify in any contract that any disputes you both (or all) cannot resolve will be turned over to the American Arbitration Association for settlement. Sometimes only a qualified outsider can come up with a solution.

Tips to Remember

- Consult an attorney and/or an accountant for guidance on the best way to buy, and run, a house—for all of you.
- A contract spelling out all of the terms of an agreement to buy, maintain, and sell a house should be drawn up in all co-buying situations in which the sharers are not married to each other.
- Consider *every* eventuality, and add that to a written agreement.

Tips to Remember

- Consult an attorney and/or an accountant for guidance on the best way to buy, and run, a house—for all of you.
- A contract spelling out all of the terms of an agreement to buy, maintain, and sell a house should be drawn up in all co-buying situations in which the sharers are not married to each other.
- Consider *every* eventuality, and add that to a written agreement.

PART II
HOW TO
COME UP WITH THAT
ELUSIVE DOWNPAYMENT

FOUR
Scrutinizing Your Own Resources

If you have been trying to save toward a downpayment, you know the scenario. You build up perhaps $3,000 and then pffft, out goes $575 for a car repair. Or one of you is laid off, and nothing can be set aside for a while.

How can you amass a downpayment? How can anyone set aside $50 or $100 a week these days? The amount of money needed is the size of the house the frustrated renter wants to buy!

As the price of homes climbs, even minimally each year, you are likely to find your goal even more elusive. When you have $6,000, you learn that you now need $9,000. Inch your savings up to $8,000, and requirements for what you are looking for now call for $11,000.

Of course, your better option is a financing program that calls for a minimal downpayment, such as loans backed by the Federal Housing Administration (FHA), and those sponsored by state housing agencies. Learn more about these in Chapter 6. You can also still find downpayments of less than 10 percent offered by a few builders (See Chapter 5). But even if you need only a minimal outlay, unless you are buying with a loan insured by the Department of Veterans Affairs (VA), which allows no downpayment, you will need *some* money.

Is it hopeless? Of course not. Saving, while certainly a commendable practice, is not the answer in this instance. You cannot save for the next ten years, while home prices and downpayment requirements keep rising so that you never catch up.

If you can afford to carry a house once you own one, and you do have some money for that 4 to 6 percent of the mortgage you will need for closing expenses, it makes more sense to buy now by really tapping every source you can for a downpayment. This is the one area of homebuying that is likely to prove most challenging, the one that will require the most work on your part. Still, the programs offering downpayment assistance are out there!

Why So
High These Days?

As you have been reading these pages, you have already given some thought to the price you want to pay, can afford to pay, or *have* to pay for a home. Let's say you estimate the price of the home at $110-120,000. Ten percent of this is at least $11,000, and lenders are requiring 10 to 20 percent down these days, unless you have help from some government program.

Leverage has always been a key term in real estate. It means buying the most you can with the smallest investment of your own money. Applied to a home, it can translate into spending $15,000 to get a $125,000 house. How could you acquire so much for so little in any other area of the marketplace? And a house is something that is going to become more valuable over the years, not depreciate instantly like a car or furniture.

This is both good and bad news these days, however. You have just read the good. The not-so-great side of the equation is that over the last several years lenders are clamping down on the money they extend for mortgages.

They insist that mortgage applicants be prepared to invest more up front. If downpayments are higher, lenders reason, homeowners in financial trouble will think twice about turning the key in the door and heading off to the Interstate. They will stay and try to work through their problems, or stay and try to sell the house. Whatever they do, they will not be handing the bank more headaches.

Lenders say there is a definite correlation between loan defaults and the amount of money a borrower has invested in the home. The lower the downpayment, the greater the risk. VA and FHA home loans usually have twice the delinquencies of conventional loans, but both of them are key sources of low downpayment financing.

Another reason for higher downpayment requirements is the existence of the secondary mortgage market (see Chapter 6). This market has demanded that mortgage lenders scrutinize downpayments far more closely than they have in the past. Here, too, it is for protection against default.

If You Are
in a Special Situation

Leveraging, putting down as little as you can, is usually the best way to go. Still, if you are self-employed, if you have a poor credit record, or if you are very young, you may want to—or have to—come up with more than the minumum a lender is requiring. You may also have to do this if you want to buy more house than you can comfortably carry. A higher downpayment can make lenders look more favorably on marginal-loan applicants, so consider the options in these pages very carefully—and push hard to make one of them work for you.

Think

First look around to see if you are sitting on cash you had not considered. Do you have stocks to sell? A life insurance policy you can borrow against (remembering in your budget the payments to bring its value back up again)? Do you have valuable silver or jewelry? What about tapping into retirement savings? Be careful here, though, of penalties and income taxes due on this money. Can you sell a car? (This depends on the car, naturally. One couple used their fancy foreign import, even though it was several years old, as an $18,000 downpayment on a $50,000 condominium. The sellers were quite happy to take the car in lieu of cash.)

If you are liquidating assets, it is best to get the money into some sort of savings account as quickly as you can. Do not wait until the day before you need a downpayment to sell your Chevy.

It's virtually never a good idea to borrow what you need as a cash advance on your credit card. Yes you have the money quickly, without bothering relatives, and you can pay the loan off each month over a long period of time, but credit card interest rates are among the highest in the lending business. And you can forget about tax deductions. If you borrow to your credit limit for a home, you will not have any advance available in the event of an emergency. Also, this borrowing will push up your debt load in relation to your gross month income, and these figures might prevent you from getting the mortgage you want—perhaps from getting any mortgage at all. Remember, lenders scrutinize would-be borrowers very carefully these days. They will know all about you.

Are you thinking about a bank loan? Personal loans carry higher interest rates than mortgages. A personal loan will also increase your debt load in the same way borrowing on a credit card will.

Lenders often ask mortgage applicants to show proof that downpayment funds have been in a bank account for three to six months. (This is why liquidating assets should start early in your househunting.) The lender wants to be assured that the funds have not been borrowed from another lender, and that the money you have ready for the house has come from a legitimate source, such as savings, a gift from your parents, or from selling some asset (keep the receipts or statements handy). If you have exhausted all of the obvious places and still need more money for a downpayment, it is time to move to Phase II.

Can the Folks Help Out?

More than 20 percent of all first-timers get some financial help from their parents or other relatives. Parents usually mean well when they offer, or are asked, to contribute to a downpayment fund. Some have thought the matter through carefully, but others let emotion get in the way of financial good sense. Maybe you will have to be the coolheaded one here, being sure that mom and dad will not seriously miss $10,000 from their own plans for the short-term. Will the money be a loan or a gift? If a loan, how long do you think they will *really* have to wait before it is repaid?

Your folks can give you $10,000 per year per parent with no tax obligation. The gift is not taxable to you, and has no negative tax consequences for them either (the gift is also not deductible for income tax purposes). If you are married, your parents can also give your spouse $10,000 per parent. Recipients need not be relatives.

Lenders are more willing to offer a mortgage when there

are no strings attached to the downpayment, as with a gift. If your parents can help you, the lender will probably ask them to sign a gift letter specifically stating that the money is a present and does not have to be repaid. If their check represents a loan, lenders will factor in that repayment plan with your other financial obligations and that will reduce the size of the loan they are willing to make. Indeed, some lenders will not make a loan if all of the buyer's downpayment is borrowed. Some require borrowers to have at least 5 percent in their own savings accounts, again to show their seriousness of purpose.

When lenders check borrowers' resources and see a sizable deposit just prior to purchasing a house, they can pretty well figure out the downpayment came from someone else. So try to deposit some money—and continue making deposits—as you are discussing all of this with your folks, and as early as your first thoughts about buying.

If your folks decide to help you, they ought to seek the advice of an accountant before writing a check. There are ways they can structure gifts and loans to make them, if not advantageous, then at least a little less painful, IRS-wise.

Gifts or loans toward a downpayment are the most common ways parents help their children buy a home. Several other options that might help you out follow in the next chapter.

Tips to Remember

- Liquidate assets and deposit these monies in a bank account as soon as possible.
- If the folks are helping out, be sure you all know whether their contribution is a gift or a loan, to avoid misunderstandings later.
- All of you should consult an accountant to learn the most advantageous way of giving or lending money.

FIVE
Other
Sources of Help

If you do not have the money you need, and cannot borrow from your parents, you have other options.

Federal Government Programs

You are probably already familiar with the acronym FHA, which refers to the Federal Housing Administration, a government agency under the umbrella of the U.S. Department of Housing and Urban Development (HUD). There is more about FHA-insured mortgages in Chapter 6. In this chapter we will concentrate on their downpayment requirements.

With an FHA-backed loan you *can* buy with downpayments of 5 percent or less. You will be required to pay mortgage insurance, however, that will cost you 3.8 percent of the loan up front (which can be financed), and monthly payments of 0.5 percent. These rates went into effect in 1991, and are designed to cut back on the number of problem loans from this agency. The program could also cut down on the number of homebuyers shopping FHA. Private mortgage insurance with conventional loans, covered later in this chapter, also calls for a monthly charge to the homebuyer, but there is no up-front fee. FHA-insured loans can still be a good deal for the first-time buyer, *after* some number crunching.

If you qualify for a VA-backed loan, you do not have to

make any downpayment. But here the loans are available only to veterans or widows or widowers of veterans who died of service-related injuries.

The Farmers Home Administration (FmHA) is not a household name, but it *can* make an owner of you. If you are looking to buy in a rural area, the FmHA also offers lower-than-market downpayment requirements and mortgage interest rates if the house you are buying will be your principal residence, is not a second home, and is situated in an area the FmHA defines as rural.

Then there are houses purchased through the Resolution Trust Corporation (RTC), which calls for 3 percent down if financial need can be proven. This agency's formula for financial need is very liberal, however. There is more about buying RTC homes in Chapter 14.

Your real estate agent can help you with all of these programs, although she might not be too familiar with FmHA. You can also call the regional office of each agency yourself.

Look to Your State

Every state offers some type of homebuying program for first-timers that features low downpayment requirements and lower-than-market interest rates. Money is available through bond programs, with the agency handling the program known as Mortgage Finance Housing or the Housing Finance Agency or some similar name.

There may be income requirements, and you will likely be restricted to certain areas of a city or town, but the program works! It is *only* for first-time buyers or those who have not purchased a home in the previous specified number of years, usually three.

Perhaps you have seen on a local TV news program,

lines of (almost always) young people on folding chairs in front of a local lending institution, waiting for its doors to open the next day. The TV reporter will tell you a new influx of bond money has become available, and these folks want to be first to apply for those loans. The money is spent that quickly!

To learn more about this program, contact your Governor's Office for the name and phone number of the mortgage finance agency in your state. One caveat: this program regularly appears to be in danger of disappearing for budgetary reasons.

Private Mortgage Insurance (PMI)

PMI is a common expense for first-time buyers. It is an insurance policy offered by several companies nationwide that allows buyers to make downpayments of 10 percent or less. The premium can be up to 1 percent of the mortgage due at closing, with annual premiums thereafter about 0.5 percent of the loan. The insurance can be dropped at a point when the lender feels its investment is safe, usually after five to seven years. *You* will have to approach the insurance company to have the policy dropped.

Lenders usually require PMI of borrowers who need 90-percent financing, virtually always of those who require 95 percent, and often for buyers applying for 80-percent loans. Unfortunately for you, insurers have been tightening their standards for PMI coverage, just as mortgage lenders have been clamping down on criteria for home financing. Here, too, you must have a good credit history to secure a policy, and seem a good risk overall.

The 5-Percent Solution

Aside from government-backed programs, some private sources still exist for 5-percent downpayments. For one, there are still a few lenders around who will allow a mortgage with this low amount down.

In tough (for them) economic times, some developers of new-home communities will also advertise a 5-percent downpayment, one or two even *no* downpayment. Developers will also, again in certain economic markets, offer houses and condominiums under a lease/purchase plan.

It could well pay you to look at new-home communities in a buyer's market. The terms here could be better than buying a resale home in the more traditional manner. If it is a strong buyer's market—and you will have to know how much leverage you have in negotiating—bargain over *everything*, a point that will be made often throughout these pages.

GE Capital Mortgage Insurance Corporation, is offering 5-percent loans. It could be worth your while to investigate, if you are flexible. After many phone calls to mortgage officers to learn more, you might strike gold.

To be a candidate for these loans you will need a whistle-clean credit history. Also, most lenders have ceased offering adjustable rate mortgages (ARMs) involving 5-percent downpayments, so you will have to secure a fixed-rate loan. The disappearance of ARMs in this instance is because they are a somewhat chancey business for lenders, and the default rate on them is higher than on fixed-rate mortgages. Add to that the riskiness overall of a 5-percent downpayment and you have *very* edgy lenders.

Lease/Purchase Programs

Renting that leads to buying can be an excellent path to homeownership, but do not waste your time trying to make such an arrangement work in a booming seller's market. They will not need you.

Here is how this works. You rent a house or condominium, signing a contract that states that at the end of six, twelve, or eighteen months you will be allowed to buy that property, at *a price set at the signing of the contract*. This protects you from ordinary price increases in the housing market each year. Another good feature: the sellers, who for the moment will be your landlords, allow you to apply some of your rent toward the purchase, which will go toward a downpayment. Naturally, there is a written agreement between all parties to seal the pact and spell out specifics.

The lease/purchase can work particularly well with new-home developers who are anxious to sell their properties and do not mind renting them initially, with the proviso that the tenant plans to buy. You should know here that your option money will not be refunded if you elect *not* to buy at the end of the specified time. Unless you can prove some sort of fraud on the part of the seller, you do not have any legal grounds for getting that money back. It must be applied toward the purchase of the house. If the real estate market goes down, you can, of course, decline to exercise your option to buy, which could be a wise decision, even though it means forfeiting the option money.

As it is in every other real estate deal, everything here is negotiable, from purchase price to such details as maintenance of the property. Naturally, you will want to consult a lawyer knowledgeable in real estate practices to represent you in contract negotiations. Be very sure that your contract stipulates whether you *can* buy at the end of a specified period of time, or whether you *must* buy.

Equity Sharing

Whether you will find equity sharing workable depends on the state of the real estate market where you intend to buy, and on the national economy. You need an investor here, and no one outside your family is likely to want to buy unless the value of your home is increasing regularly. Mom and dad are more likely to tolerate little or no return on their investment in your house.

Shared equity deals can be arranged in a number of ways. Most commonly, an investor (known as the owner-investor) provides the downpayment and even the closing costs. The buyer (known as the owner-occupant) lives in the home, makes the monthly mortgage payments, and pays for maintenance. Both names are on the deed.

At the end of a specified period (usually five years), the home is sold. But if you want to stay in the house, you can refinance the loan. The owner-investor receives the original downpayment and any closing costs he or she paid from the proceeds of the sale. If there is a profit, the two parties split it.

What if there is no profit? Sometimes the agreement is extended by both parties another two or three years in the hope that values will rise. But some investors do sell at a loss.

The Internal Revenue Service recognizes equity sharing. Internal Revenue Code 280A authorizes that form of co-ownership, requiring a written contract between co-owners. There is no *standard* contract, however, and both owners can seek the advice of an attorney or financial planner to draw up the appropriate papers. Among other points, a contract should specify

- title ownership by all of the parties involved;
- the percentage of the property owned by each buyer;
- a buy-out arrangement, so that if one of you wants to sell, the other can buy out that share at a reasonable cost;
- how profits are to be split (most commonly after the sale of the property in five years);
- how disputes are to be resolved, perhaps through arbitration;
- payment by the resident of any capital improvements he or she wants, such as a pool or a porch;
- cost splitting between both owners of expenses that exceed $1,000; and
- a rental contract for the owner-occupant to rent the owner-investor's share of the house if the investor wants to deduct depreciation on his or her share of the property.

How you decide the above stipulations is between you and the owner-investor.

You have already read about the nervous attitude of lenders these days when they consider extending credit to home buyers. Well, they view equity sharing deals as risky, too, because the loans have become difficult to sell on the secondary market. Still, some lenders do carry financing they do not sell to the secondary market. They will probably demand a high downpayment, perhaps 25 percent, and some will require that the owner-occupant's income be the only one to qualify for the loan. Previously, many lenders had used the combined incomes of the investor and occupant to determine qualification. You may also find you will be quoted a higher interest rate and might have to pay points on your loan.

Your real estate agent should be able to direct you to a company that will put together the equity sharing arrangement for you—at a cost of about $500—or you might be able to secure all of the help you need from a lawyer specializing in real estate.

Tips to Remember

- Check federal and state government programs for low downpayment requirements.
- Be aware of the real estate market, both nationally and locally, so that you know how much leverage you have. Some programs that could benefit you will be no help at all in a lively seller's market.
- Look carefully at mortgage insurance fees—both private mortgage insurance and insurance with FHA-backed loans. You will have to add these expenses to the carrying costs of a home.

PART III
HOW TO
NAIL DOWN A MORTGAGE

SIX
Your Financing Options

"But don't I find the house first, and then think about the mortgage?" Actually, this would be working backward. If you were purchasing, say, a new television set, you would look over your finances first, wouldn't you? You would have to think how you will pay for it, weighing credit card against personal check. Or perhaps you are one of those renegade consumers who pays for major purchases with cash.

Although you might have *looked* at television sets for quite some time, you cannot tell a sales clerk "I'll take that one" until you figure out how you will pay for it.

It is the same with a home. If you do not know, within a certain range, how much house you can afford, and how you plan to pay for it, then how can you know to narrow down your search to specifically priced homes? How can you negotiate over price?

It is wise not to begin serious househunting until you know about mortgages, and in fact have been prequalified by a mortgage lender. Indeed, most real estate agents will hustle you off to a lender before showing you homes. They do not want to waste their time with "browsers" who might not be able to secure a loan. They also do not want to antagonize their sellers by bringing them would-be buyers who are, in terms of actually purchasing that property, unknown quantities.

Words to Borrow By

Since this is a new field for you, here are some common terms you will hear as you progress through various home borrowing stages.

Mortgage. Simply, it is a loan that is secured by real property. If you do not pay back the loan as agreed, you lose the property. Naturally, in practice it is not quite this simple. The complexity of foreclosure procedures has, in fact, stimulated the creation of a type of financing where failure to pay can mean rather quick eviction and loss of your home. It is called the trust deed.

The Deed of Trust, or Trust Deed. This is not a mortgage because you cannot pledge property that you do not own as security for a loan. When you finance through a deed of trust, you do not take title to your home. The deed, which is the legal instrument that grants title to the property, is held by a third party (not by the lender or borrower). Usually that is the title insurance company or the escrow company that handles the closing. Here, if you default in your loan, the results are invariably faster than mortgage foreclosures. Your home might be offered for sale in just ninety days following the default. For simplicity, the word *mortgage* is being used throughout this book, but do find out exactly which instrument is used in your state.

Mortgagor and Mortgagee. The lender of the money is the mortgagee, the borrower is the mortgagor.

Who Offers Mortgages?

You do not want to walk into the bank where you have your checking account and Holiday Club and take whatever mortgage terms they have to offer. It will pay you—perhaps thousands of dollars over the life of the loan—to shop around for mortgage terms. They are *not* the same with every institution. However, it would be wise to *start* with the bank that has your savings and/or checking accounts, in that lenders do give preferential treatment to their longtime customers.

A variety of sources lend money for home loans: mutual savings banks and savings and loan associations, commercial banks, credit unions, finance companies (those affiliated with or wholly owned by large real estate agencies or franchises), government agencies, mortgage bankers (companies that qualify applicants, find the best available loans, fund the initial loan, and then sell to or place that loan with another lender or investor), mortgage brokers (a person or company who, for a fee, will find a lender), and home sellers.

A Variety of Loans

There are government-backed loans and conventional loans, where no government agency is involved. In addition, there is seller financing, where sellers offer mortgages to buyers, usually for a limited time of three to five years, whereupon the buyer secures more traditional financing. Seller financing works only in the most severe buyers' market, where property after property remains unsold for months, perhaps years. Or when a seller is particularly eager to move right this very moment and cannot wait for a few months while his house goes through the ordinary selling channels.

Here are the most popular conventional loans. The fixed-term, X-percent loan has traditionally been the most popular of loans. The life of the mortgage can be 15, 20, 25, or 30 years at an interest rate that remains the same for the duration of the loan. A fixed-rate, 15-year term loan, for example, might carry a lower interest rate than a 30-year loan, but the monthly payments are higher because the principal is being paid off twice as fast.

The adjustable-rate loan (ARM) offers a "teaser" low interest rate at the outset of the mortgage that can be three or more points lower than a fixed-rate loan, but this figure can rise dramatically after the first year, and steadily thereafter.

The interest rates lenders charge for ARMs are pegged to an independent financial index they select. There are many indexes, carrying a variety of components. To protect homebuyers from large rate increases, most lenders set limits on the amount rates may fluctuate when it is time for a loan's interest rate to be determined. This is known as the adjustable rate cap. With a lifetime cap, lenders set a ceiling and floor for rate increases and decreases over the life of an ARM. The lifetime cap is expressed either as a particular percentage rate, or as five to seven percentage points over or under that initial rate. Be *sure* to ask about caps when you inquire about ARM.

Under government-backed loans there is the Federal Housing Administration's FHA-insured loans, both fixed-rate and adjustable, and the Department of Veterans Affairs' VA-backed loans, available to servicemen and women, and widows and widowers of servicepeople who died while on duty. Both of these have low or no down-payment requirements, and offer other benefits to buyers. There is also the little-known Farmers Home Administration, which offers FHA-guaranteed loans to those buying homes in rural areas.

A growing number of borrowers these days are opting for 15-year loans in place of the more traditional 30-year term, both to build equity faster and to save thousands of dollars in finance charges. These loans may be a little harder to secure than the 30-year terms because the monthly payments are higher, which translates into your having to earn more money to qualify. Your payments are *not* 50-percent higher than with 30-year mortgages. They are usually only 20 to 30 percent above that amount, because more of each monthly payment goes toward principal instead of interest.

You will also come upon "balloon" mortgages. When you take on a balloon loan, you agree to make a fixed monthly payment that will amortize your loan over, say, thirty years. You might pay interest only on the loan, but then on a specified date—five, seven, ten, or any predetermined number of years in the future—the entire unpaid balance of the loan becomes due and payable. You must pay up, refinance, or lose the property.

Balloon mortgages can keep monthly housing costs down if you are rather certain of a company transfer, or plan to move anyway, well within the period of the balloon. Otherwise, be wary when you see the words *balloon payment*.

Similarly, if you plan to pull up stakes after just three or four years in the house you will buy, you might want to choose the attractive initial rates of the ARM, so that you are gone from that house before the rate begins its upward spiral. Or you might choose the ARM if fixed-rate loans are carrying a high interest rate at the time you are buying.

If you intend to stay in the house for an indeterminate number of years, but certainly more than three or five, and if interest rates are low at the moment, your choice will probably be the fixed-rate loan. The longer you plan to stay in your house, the more it makes sense to pay discount points to lower your interest rate (points are usually tax deductible).

Some additional notes:

• Buying a fixer-upper? Be sure to check state (Mortgage Finance Agency) and federal government agencies (FHA, VA) to see if there is fix-up help available at the time you are buying. The FHA, for example, offers the excellent 203(k) program, where you can secure just one mortgage loan to finance both buying and rehabilitating the property.

• A very smart move would be to purchase a small paperback book that can go by a variety of names (Mortgage Payments, Mortgage Calculator Guide), is printed by a number of different publishers, costs about $5.00, and contains nothing but figures. Used by lenders and real estate agents, the book can be invaluable to house shoppers. It can tell you just by running your finger across a page what a $100,000 mortgage will cost you each month if it is a 30-year loan at 9 percent, if it is a 15-year loan at 9 percent, and so on.

• Check mortgage brokers for "alternative financing"—programs for borrowers with special problems, such as high debt-to-income ratio.

What to Ask Lenders

When you call potential lenders, have a list of questions you want to ask them written out and by your side. Ask for the mortgage department, or a mortgage loan officer. You will want to know the following:

• *What types of financing do you have available now?* Does the lender offer both fixed-rate and adjustable plans? Are

FHA and VA mortgages available? What other plans does this particular institution have to offer?

• *How long a term are you willing to offer for each type of loan?* You will want to know if the term is fixed on adjustable rate loans, and whether there is a lower rate of interest for shorter-term loans.

• *Can ARMs be converted to fixed-rate loans at some point?* If so, at what cost and rate?

• *What guidelines do you use for loan qualifications?* How you can interpret the response follows later in this chapter, under "How Much Can You Borrow?"

• *What is your minimum downpayment requirement for each type of loan?*

• *Do you charge points?* You will want to know how many for each type of loan.

• *Is there a loan origination fee?*

• *Is there an application fee?* How much? Remember, these are nonrefundable and cannot be applied to any other expense.

• *Can you give me a rough estimate of closing costs?*

• *Is there a prepayment penalty on any of the loans?* This is important if you think you might be transferred and will have to move sooner than you plan.

• *Do you offer preferred customer benefits?* Some lenders lower the interest rates on mortgage loans if the borrower makes use of other banking services being offered— savings accounts, checking accounts, CDs and money market accounts, and so on.

• *How long will a mortgage decision take after an application is made?* Three to five weeks is common in a busy market, less in a slow one.

• *How long will a mortgage commitment be effective?* Some lenders will make a commitment for ninety days, with renewals available. Some will make commitments for up to six months, especially on new construction.

• *Does the interest rate remain constant on the loan commitment?* Some lenders will be willing to give a commitment for a mortgage loan, but that loan will be written at the interest rate prevailing *at the time of closing,* which can be somewhat risky for you in a time of fluctuating rates. Other lenders will guarantee the rate, but if rates go down before you close, will hold you to the original rate. To get a better deal, you will have to begin mortgage shopping again. Finally, there is the best deal of all, which is just that. Some lenders will guarantee the "best" rate. If interest rates go up before your closing date, they will stay with the rate at which they made their commitment to you. If rates are down by your closing, however, they will write your mortgage loan at the lower rate.

Getting an attractive interest rate locked in is, as you can see, a ticklish business, but an important one and one that you must understand as you begin shopping for a loan. You can write for a free fourteen-page booklet from the Federal Reserve Board that will help. It's titled *A Consumer's Guide to Mortgage Lock-Ins,* and is available from the Federal Reserve Board at 20th and C Streets NE, Washington, DC 20551.

• *What's new?* Many lenders inaugurate, from time to time, special mortgage plans for that institution only. No doubt the officer to whom you talk will mention these programs, perhaps even open the conversation with them. If not, it cannot hurt to ask if that institution has any new mortgage packages on the horizon.

You should talk to at least six lenders. This will help you analyze and compare effectively. A cautionary note, however: a few could quote attractive rates over the phone; then, when you make an application, you find the rates have risen. How to overcome the practice, if it does exist where you are? Lock in the rate you want, as discussed earlier. Also, be sure you are getting comparative quotes on the same loans. There are too many variations on rates to go into them all in these pages, but to take one example, you might be given one quote on a 30-year, fixed-rate loan. But this might really mean that the lender offers a 30-year loan with a fixed rate for the first seven years, with a lower interest rate for those first seven years, then a balloon payment or refinancing at prevailing rates due at the end of that time for the final twenty-three years. See how narrowly defined programs can be? And how there can be programs within programs?

How Much Can You Borrow?

Typically, renters should allot 25 to 30 percent of their income to rent. If you're paying more, your landlord doesn't care if you have to scrimp in other areas—just as long as you meet your obligations to him every month.

Not so with mortgage lenders. They will be sure that your mortgage is only what they feel you can afford. If they are willing to offer you a mortgage for $110,000, and you need $130,000 for the home you want, you will have to make up the difference by coming up with another $20,000 for the downpayment.

Ten or fifteen years ago, most lenders would go by the gross annual income formula. For example, if you made $30,000 a year, you could get a mortgage loan of $60,000. Today, lenders who still use that formula, and they are mostly small, hometown institutions, allow 2½ or even 3 times gross annual income.

Then there is the income to housing costs formula. In this qualification procedure, the anticipated housing expenses are computed. These include mortgage payment, real estate taxes, fire and catastrophe insurance, and mortgage insurance, if any. To qualify with many lenders, your total monthly figure for housing expenses must not exceed 28 percent of your gross monthly income (some lenders will go slightly higher). For example, if you gross $3,000 a month, your housing expenses should not exceed $840.

Another criterion is the income to long-term debt payment formula. Rather than monthly housing costs alone, here all of the borrower's long-term (ten months or more) debt payments are calculated. Included are car payments, large outstanding charge account balances, child support and alimony payments, and college loans. To qualify with most lenders, the total monthly payment for housing expenses *and* long-term debts should not exceed 36 to 39 percent of gross monthly income. These guidelines will give you 8 percent or more for other debt besides housing expenses.

As you work the numbers to see how much mortgage you can probably afford, keep in mind that a mortgage lender is not concerned with the fact that you need a new car, or plan to return to school for some postgraduate training, or have no furniture for the home you buy. Mortgage lenders are only interested in protecting their investment. So you can see that ultimately *you* must decide how much of your income you can commit to housing, taking many factors into consideration.

Tips to Remember

- Owning is not like renting in that you will not be able to buy *anything* you like. A mortgage lender, unlike a landlord, will be sure you buy only what that institution thinks you can comfortably afford.
- Call several lenders so that you can compare mortgage terms. They are *not* all alike.
- Give some thought to how long you might stay in this house. That can help you with the mortgage you choose.
- Call government agencies for their programs, especially if you are buying a fixer-upper and need rehabilitation money. They might be able to help.

SEVEN

Preparing to Apply for a Loan

Now you are ready to apply for a mortgage. Gulp.

Yes, this is one of life's more dramatic—and traumatic—moments. But remember, mortgage lenders are in the business of lending money for mortgages. They *want* to help you. In certain economies they are even *dying* to lend money.

Having a document from a lender, stating that that institution will offer you a mortgage of X dollars, will help you look like the serious buyer you are. It is also a good negotiating tool: no eager seller is going to quickly turn away a qualified buyer. Finally, putting together the material you need early will allow you to clear up any errors or discrepancies so that what you ultimately present to a mortgage lender looks good—and good translates into approved.

Prequalifying, or being offered a "conditional" mortgage, is almost, but not quite, as good as an actual loan. The principal ingredient missing from the lender's file is still a signed contract for the house you want to buy. Once you have that in hand, you can, if the lender considers that property a sound investment for that institution, be offered a true mortgage. Note that prepurchase commitments will differ among lenders. The better programs are contingent only on a satisfactorily signed sales contract and appraisal. *You* do not have to do any more qualifying.

There are many factors, as you will see, that enter into being approved for a home loan. Some you cannot change, but with other points you can, legally, work to make yourself look good, or at least better than you seem now.

The Paper Chase

If you saw a bit of paperwork with the downpayment—perhaps a shared-equity agreement, a 'gift letter' from your parents—now you will be flooded. Papers, documents, files, numbers—whew! But you can be organized and prepared for the mortgage application, rather than scrambling around for different bits of information as you learn they will be needed.

Income, debt, downpayment, and a good credit report are the prime components lenders use as a gauge of creditworthiness. From that information they will come up with an amount they would be willing to lend you. Perhaps you will learn that you need to pay off some old bills, or clean up your credit, or save still more. Whatever lenders pass on to you in the way of tips will help move you along through the mortgage approval process.

Not every lender will require all of the following papers. Also, it is a good idea to take the mortgage application form home with you, to give it the attention it warrants, and not fill it out at the lending institution. Ask for a few copies. Use one as a rough draft, making all of the changes you need on that form. Then the final copy, in ink or typed, will be as neat and correction-free as possible. You will not want the lender to see a form with scratched-out figures, or dabs of correction fluid here and there. Besides looking messy, it could make the lender wonder about the veracity of the information it contains.

You will need the following information to start this process:

• *Addresses.* Where you have lived for the past two years.

• *Assets.* Your holdings such as stocks and bonds (if you have an account with a stock brokerage firm, include the most recent statement), IRAs, vested amounts in retirement plans, surrender value of life insurance policies, cars, and so on. List current balances, names and addresses of institutions, and account numbers for each item. Remember to sell early such assets as jewelry, a second car, collections, and so on, that you plan to use toward the downpayment, so that your bank balance reflects as long a history of savings as possible. Lenders do not just ask for your bank balance; they also ask for the average balance for the past three to six months.

• *Debts.* Make a list of your credit cards, auto loans, school loans, and other debts. Show the name of the organization that has extended credit to you, the address, your account number, the amount owed, and the monthly payments. Money is, of course, tight with you just now, as you try to set aside funds for a downpayment and closing costs. Still, if you can, pay off as many bills as possible, to reduce your debt load. Not carrying too much debt is an important factor in your being approved for a loan.

• *Marital Status.* Divorced? Collect the pertinent papers that may be needed by the lender. You can elect to show alimony and/or child support papers to help you obtain the largest possible mortgage.

• *Extra Income.* If you have *regular* sources of extra income, add these to your application.

• *Foreclosure and Bankruptcy.* If you experienced either within the previous ten years, you must report that information to the lender.

• *Gift Letter.* If mom and dad have helped you with the downpayment, be sure to have a letter from them attesting to that, noting that the money is indeed a gift and they do not expect to be repaid.

• *Income and Employment Records.* Collect W-2 statements for the past two years, and pay stubs from the previous month. Incidentally, this is not a good time to change jobs, unless the new position will be in the same line of work and you will be earning more money. A lender will be skeptical of too much job hopping, especially if the changes were not really promotions, or if they involved a total career switch.

• *Social Security Numbers.* For you and anyone buying with you.

• *Tax Returns.* Only for the self-employed. You will need returns for the past two years.

• *VA Documentation.* If you are applying for a VA-backed loan you will need a certificate of eligibility. To obtain that form, you can contact your local VA office six to eight weeks before applying for a loan.

Your Credit Report

A vitally important element in your being approved for a loan is what your credit report says about you. If you have no idea, it is wise to send for a copy now, before a lender sees it, so that you can clear up any errors.

Check the Yellow Pages under Credit Reporting Agencies to find the one that has you on file. You can expect to pay anywhere from $2 to $20 for a copy of your report, and you should not have to wait more than a few days for it to arrive once the credit bureau receives your check. If you have just recently been denied credit for one reason or another, you are entitled to a copy of your file at no cost to you.

In this document you will find bill-paying information

about you: When and how promptly you have paid credit cards, department store charges, auto loans, and the like. It is not, as many consumers mistakenly believe, a rating service. Credit bureaus attach no rating to those they list; they merely collect data and pass it on upon request.

Go over everything in that report carefully. If you see an account where you have made a recent payment and it has not yet been recorded, bring along with you to the mortgage loan officer a copy of your cancelled check to that store or credit card company.

If you find an outright mistake in your report, write to the source of the erroneous data and clear up the matter with them. Work with the credit bureau until you are satisfied that the mistake has been corrected.

Give yourself plenty of time—credit bureaus can work slowly. Actually, these days consumers are complaining of so many mistakes in their reports from sources with poor record-keeping methods that you should allow at least a month between securing your credit report and approaching a lender. You do not know what you will find in that document, no matter how religiously you have paid your bills.

Dealing with a Poor Credit History, Including Bankruptcy

Maybe you know, reading this, that your credit report is going to be a mess. There will be delinquencies and difficulties you cannot fix because they are correct. Now what do you do?

Be prepared. Were you delinquent in paying bills for four months in 1990 because you had just been laid off? Because you had serious surgery? Was there a death in the family? A divorce? You can send a letter of explanation to the credit bureau and ask them to affix it to your report to serve as an explanation for anyone requesting your file. Be prepared to offer that explanation to the mortgage loan officer, as well, so that he or she is prepared for the credit report's bad news. Copies of doctors' bills can help document long illnesses.

If you had a dispute with a credit card company over a payment, and that is still being worked out in correspondence, bring copies of those letters with you to the lender.

If you have no explanation for the six months or one year or two years of late payments, you will just have to work around that black mark. You can explain to the mortgage loan officer that you are now more responsible about your debts and—your ace in the hole—that you can make a larger downpayment than would ordinarily be required.

Another option: a mortgage financed by the seller of the home you want to buy. Sellers often do not check buyers' creditworthiness because, they feel, they can always foreclose in the event of mortgage nonpayment. Or pick up an assumable loan that requires no qualifying at all. You will see these advertised as such, since assumable no-qualifying can be quite a sales inducement.

To reassure a lender, you might suggest a pledged account. This means the lending institution will have extra collateral available in a third-party escrow account in case of your nonpayment. Funds supplied by you equal to three or four months of your mortgage payment are placed in the account. This can be done by the seller or any other third party to the sale, such as a title company—maybe even your employer, if you do not mind going outside your immediate circle.

The escrow instructions will state that this money is to be used only for any delinquent loan payments and late fees for the first three years of the loan. If the loan is in good standing at the end of that time, the funds, plus any interest accrued, will be returned to you. You can supply money to this fund, or another type of collateral, such as stocks, bonds, or certificates of deposit.

The lease with an option to buy is a good way to ease your way into ownership, and you can build a good credit report with prompt rental payments. Finding a mortgage co-signer (who is likely to be mom and dad) is also an option.

Finally, if you know you will have trouble securing a mortgage, you can approach mortgage brokers who apply for you to any number of lenders around the country. You will probably have to pay a somewhat higher interest rate, but if all goes well, you can refinance later. However, beware of interest rates approaching usury level that some firms charge applicants who carry a less than perfect credit rating. No matter how bad your financial situation appears on paper, you can, and should, shop around for home financing at terms you can live with.

Bankruptcy is, of course, more serious than late payments. If you can afford to buy a home now, however, do not let that credit blot keep you from approaching mortgage loan officers. There are, legally, no time limits on how soon you can secure a conventional mortgage after filing. Some lenders may turn you down no matter how far back the bankruptcy was, but others will lend within just two years of your filing. With FHA-insured loans, a bankruptcy must be discharged for at least one year; the Department of Veterans Affairs insists on a two-year wait. When applying for a home loan in this instance, you must anticipate the following:

- a lot of shopping around among lenders;
- telling the truth about your situation, and appearing apologetic and remorseful, not cavalier or casual;
- giving an explanation of what caused the bankruptcy;

- the need for a scrupulously clean credit report since the bankruptcy; and
- a sizable downpayment, perhaps 20 percent or more.

Keep in mind that if you have charged nothing since a bankruptcy, you had better build up a credit record by charging inexpensive items or taking out small loans and then repaying them promptly. If a lender sees *no* repayment record, that institution will not know if you can now handle debt.

In dealing with lenders when you have had credit problems, keep in mind the words of one mortgage loan officer: "The important thing is to be honest and open with us and to have a good explanation for what happened. We don't like surprises." Focus on the last four words. Banks and other lenders are ultraconservative institutions. The unexpected makes them scowl.

Overall

What you are striving for here is to show as much in savings as you can muster, and as few debts as possible. Pay off as many bills as you can before applying for a loan. And, as mentioned above, convert as many assets to cash as you can to build up a lean savings account. Put off major purchases until you have that mortgage nailed down.

Have answers ready for any point that does not look good on your application. If you have changed jobs frequently, for instance, prepare to explain to the lender that each was a move up, in higher salary or expanded experience. If there are snags in your credit history, be able to explain them.

When you have a thick file of material you need for your

loan application, and a short time later are handed a commitment for a loan, you can start seriously looking at houses and actually be ready to buy one.

Tips to Remember

- Prequalifying will ease your mind about what you can afford—and whether you will get a mortgage for that amount. Don't skip this step. (You may not be able to, in any event. Serious real estate agents may not want to show you homes without some idea of whether you *can* buy.)
- Be prepared to explain any black marks or puzzling data in your credit or work histories.
- Have as much in liquid savings as you can muster when you are applying for a loan.
- The lender *will* check.

PART IV
HOW TO HOUSEHUNT KNOWING ALL OF YOUR OPTIONS

EIGHT
Househunting with and Without an Agent

Now that you know how much house you can afford, you are ready for serious house shopping. At this point you need help in further crystallizing your housing needs.

Using a Real Estate Agent

By all means take advantage of the many services offered by real estate agencies. They will cost you nothing because, except in special situations, it is the seller of the house who pays the real estate salesperson's fee. Househunters, especially first-timers, are foolish if they do not use these professionals' help. While there are certainly some cautions in this area, a knowledgeable realty agent can direct you to the pool of properties likely to interest *you*, and away from totally unacceptable houses that will only waste your time and energy.

A word here about who's who in this field. A real estate broker is any person, firm, or corporation that, for a fee or commission, seeks to sell, buy, exchange, or lease real property. Every state has strict laws for licensing brokers. Only a licensed broker can enter into a contract to act as an agent in handling real property. The real estate office you visit is owned by a broker.

A person licensed by the state to work in real estate is the real estate salesperson, sometimes called an agent. Salespersons cannot enter into a contract to see property, act in any agency capacity, or collect a commission for their work; those roles are reserved for the broker, under whose supervision they work. In practice, most of the people who will show you homes are salespersons. Because *agent* is the more common usage for all of those folks selling real estate, that term will be used throughout this book for both brokers and salespersons.

Realtor is another word you will come across frequently. It is also often used, incorrectly, to refer to anyone who sells real estate. Actually, the word is a registered trademark of the National Association of Realtors (NAR), the trade organization.

Whether a broker or salesperson, these folks can provide you with help in several phases of the buying process:

• *Qualifying for a Mortgage*. Perhaps you have already been qualified by a mortgage lender. Some folks go straight to the real estate agent for the number crunching, but to avoid strain and surprises, you would do better to work with lending institutions before serious househunting begins. You can tell, or show, the real estate agent just what the mortgage lender you have chosen has done for you in the way of qualifying.

In some instances the real estate agent will be plugged into a lending institution you did not call. Maybe she (most residential agents are women) can steer you to a good financing package, if you do not already have a commitment.

In any event, be open with your agent about your bad credit report, or your mere three months at your present job, or any other fact in your past or present that could work against you in buying. She will listen (she has heard it all before) and try to turn negative data into a positive buyer profile. She needs the sale.

• *Supplying Local Information.* Every real estate agent should know her geographical territory extremely well. Information on property taxes, schools, neighborhoods, recreation facilities, and so on should be on the tip of her tongue. Use her knowledge to help you choose among towns and from one neighborhood to another within a town.

• *Offering Maps and Printed Information.* If you ask, most agents will offer you a street map of the area in which they sell. That will be invaluable for drive-by tours without her and for poking around surrounding regions. Many local nonprofit organizations (the newcomers club, the library, the League of Women Voters) leave flyers and newsletters in real estate offices. Take them home and read them. They will give you a more personal insight into the area that interests you.

• *Using Multiple Listing Service Tools.* The orderly arrangement of listing sheets on nearly all the property that is for sale in a given community, by price, with pictures and with all pertinent sales information, is the hallmark of Multiple Listing Services across the country. If you work with a real estate office that belongs to such a service, your househunt will be still less tiring, and a lot more thorough. Ask the real estate agent to see the listing books. Go through the pictures. You may see something that interests you that the agent may not have thought would, but most of all you will be sure you have not missed anything.

• *Offering Comparables.* One of the best services an agent can provide is telling buyers at what price similar properties have recently sold. Most real estate agencies have such information on file. Ask to see the "comparables book" or "comparables file" as you begin to narrow down your search to one particular neighborhood. These listings of houses that have sold within the past year, with both asking price and actual selling price shown on the page, should prevent you from overpaying.

• *Evaluating Properties*. You can expect your agent to have inspected a property before showing it to you, although this is not always possible with brand-new listings. She should be able to answer your questions about the neighborhood, the lot, floor plan, and so on. After she has been working with you for a while, the agent should know your preferences and eliminate undesirable properties without dragging you out to see them.

A Few Words About Disclosure

There are two major areas of homebuying where the word *disclosure* has been cropping up regularly in the last few years. The first is the real estate agents' disclosing to would-be buyers that they represent the seller. Many buyers do not know that extremely important fact about the buying process. The seller pays the agent's commission from proceeds from the sale of the house. Agents' loyalties are with the seller, although they may very well be genuinely helpful to you and sincerely interested in your finding a home you like.

Because of this relationship with the seller, while you should certainly tell the real estate agent all you can about your financial situation and mortgage application, and what you need and want in a home, there is one thing you should not disclose: exactly how much you will pay for a home. You have been qualified, so both you and the agent know the price range where you are shopping, but do not be any more definite than "We want to look at something costing no less than, say, $95,000 and no more than $110,000." You do not want to give away your bargaining hand by telling the seller to the specific dollar what you will spend.

The second use of the word *disclosure* refers to agent and seller bringing any problems with the house to the attention of buyers, hiding nothing. Disclosure can also apply to a seller's or agent's knowledge of plans for the community, or the street on which the house stands, that could also turn off a prospective buyer.

Just how much an agent—and to a greater extent the seller—should disclose is still being weighed, both in the profession and in courts. In any event, you cannot afford to passively accept what agents say—or don't say—and move on to the next buying stage. Poke around on your own, to be sure the many questions raised in these chapters are answered to your satisfaction.

Finding the Right Agent

It could take some time. If you are seriously considering several towns in your region, you will probably need a different agent for each, in that an agent's knowledge of her turf is one of the major benefits of her service. You will also want someone with whom you feel comfortable and whom you trust. Of course, you want a knowledgeable, hardworking person, too.

Once you find that person, stick with her. In areas where multiple listing is commonly used, your agent can show you any property advertised by any multiple listing member office. When you see another office's ad in the newspaper for the property that you think might interest you, call your agent. She will probably have information about it and will be able to take you there. Even when a property is not listed on a multiple listing service, most brokers are happy to co-broke—that is, allow another agent to show their listing for a split commission.

By remaining loyal to your agent you will save yourself countless phone calls from every agent who gets your name. You can also save yourself a lawsuit. This is rare, of course, and certainly drastic, but here is how one could happen: You see a home showed to you by agent X and decide no, that is not for you. Three weeks later, agent Y convinces you to look at it again. Well, gee, now it looks better somehow. You buy it. The first agent sues. The legal question is: Does the first agent deserve part of the commission? The answer is often yes, but each case is decided individually, and court time can delay a sale. Do you want the aggravation?

Loyalty, however, does not make sense if you feel your agent is not doing the best job for you. If that's so, leave her and find another. This is a major, major purchase and you need the best.

The best method for finding a good agent is through personal referral. Ask friends who have recently purchased a home. Another good strategy is reading the large display classified ads in your local paper, where real estate offices congratulate top sellers. Call one of those selling stars and make an appointment for an interview.

Attending open houses may be an activity you are used to by now. Talking with the agent stationed there for the day incurs no obligation on your part, and may yield one with whom you can work.

Two of the more chancy methods of finding an agent are calling an office in response to an ad you have seen, and walking into an office and saying you want to buy a home. Most realty offices assign their agents "floor time." Any prospect who calls in response to advertising, or comes in from the street, during that time is the floor agent's customer. Unfortunately, floor time is not based on competence. A slight improvement on that poor strategy is asking for the listing agent for the property in the ad you have noted. This will at least direct you to the person who knows all about the home that interests you.

Avoid working with relatives, if you can, unless they are award-winning salespeople. Also, skip part-time agents. You want someone who works full-time, who is there when listings come in and who is always "plugged in." Part-timers just cannot be.

The Buyer's Broker

This is a small but growing trend on the homebuying landscape: real estate agents who represent the buyer. Buyer's brokers can be especially effective when acting for you in "for sale by owner" home sales. By all means look into how these agents work in your area, but consider these points first.

• Buyer's brokers can represent buyers, sellers and buyers at different times, or both parties at the same time. Go with what is known as exclusive agencies. This means no conflict of interest. Be very sure that any buyer's broker you engage is working just for *you*.
• Try to avoid signing an exclusive contract, which means that you cannot simultaneously work with other agents, and possibly that you have to pay a commission to the buyer's broker if you find a "for sale by owner" (known as FSBO and pronounced fizbo) house. Ask many questions before signing, such as your finding a home on your own, and, of course, what happens if you work on your own with a home being marketed by the seller. Limit the term of the contract, and ask for a thirty-day escape

clause to give you an out if you are dissatisfied with the service.

• Cost? You may be asked for a retainer of several hundred dollars, to be refunded when you purchase a home through that buyer's broker. You could be charged a flat fee, or there could be a fifty-fifty commission split between the seller's broker and your broker. You can negotiate for the lowest flat fee available, and then ask the seller to pay it, because he or she expects to pay an agent's commission anyway. Or you could go with the commission, and ask the seller to absorb that as well. The difference between the two could be slight, but the commission might spur on the buyer's broker. FSBO sellers usually agree to pay the buyer's broker half the customary real estate sales commission. Just know that all of this is negotiable, particularly in a slow market.

There are still only a few buyer's brokers in many parts of the country. If you are interested, you can call, toll-free, the Buyers Resource, Consumer Advocate Division, (located in Denver) at 1–800–359–4092 for the names and addresses of agents in your community.

A Few Words About Discrimination

It does still exist, of course, despite governmental, professional, and civic efforts. Race is the most obvious basis for discrimination, but religion, national origin, sex, marital status, children in the family, and several other factors may predispose an agent to show—or not show—certain properties to certain people. Such activity is called steering, and it is against the law.

If you feel that you are being steered, for a reason other than your ability to afford the house in question, you can change the situation. If the agent in question is a member of the National Association of Realtors, call or write your local Realtor Board first. You can find it in the white pages of the phone book, or in the Yellow Pages where real estate agents run their advertisements. In the corner of some of the larger ads there is likely to be a line such as "Member, Upstate Country Board of Realtors."

If not satisfied with their reaction, you might contact the National Association of Realtors, 430 North Michigan Avenue, Chicago, Illinois 60611. Their phone number is (312) 329–8200. An investigation will follow. In the meantime, continue your efforts to find a home by using independent brokers not associated with any professional group.

If you wish to take your action against discriminatory practices further, you can notify your state real estate commission. Proven cases of discrimination can result in suspension or loss of license for the agent involved. Sometimes just the *threat* of reporting these practices can put a stop to them.

Another source of advice is your local Community Housing Resources Board.

Making the Househunt Easier

Even working with a real estate agent, you will need some system to your search to keep from short-circuiting from all you have seen and heard.

First, be sure the agent knows the type of home you want, which is different from the price range and architectural style. Specify absolute needs, such as three bedrooms.

Limit yourself to viewing no more than six to eight properties in one town in one day. Beyond that number, features will become blurred in your mind and fatigue will affect your perceptions. Similarly, give a day to each town if you are interested in several. Don't keep crisscrossing back and forth from Pleasantville to Pleasant Cove. By concentrating on separate towns on separate days you will get a good idea of comparative value.

By all means drive around in the agent's car. Chauffeuring is also her business. While she is driving, you can take notes, mark your street map or just take in the view. Following the agent in your own car is also not a good idea. Being with her allows you to ask questions as they occur. You can always talk privately back at home, or on the drive home.

Househunting Without an Agent

While you are driving around with an agent you will notice several For Sale by Owner signs in front of properties that might also interest you. There is no harm in calling those sellers and arranging to see the homes.

The biggest problem with FSBO's is overpricing by the owner. Most people love their homes, and everyone wants to make a killing in real estate. Sometimes the seller has no idea of what comparable homes in his neighborhood are selling for and simply comes up with a figure that would make him happy. It is often, alas, well over what similar houses in his neighborhood are fetching.

When you call about FSBO ads, ask the price and the street address (you will already know that if you are following up on a sign in front of the property). Let the seller talk about the number of rooms, special features, and the like. It is all right to give your name. The seller will feel more comfortable. If the house is one you have not seen, tell the seller you will call him back if you want to go through it. If you do not know exactly where the house is, get out your street map and track it down.

Going through FSBOs can be awkward for both parties. The seller points out niceties and the buyer generally mumbles. Ask questions. What are the taxes? Why are you selling? Where does that ladder lead? But say nothing about the condition of the house, or the asking price, at this stage. And, whatever you do, do not in any way remark negatively on the sellers' taste in furnishings, or put down any extra touches they have added to the house. They will be insulted and you may do yourself out of a sale if you want that home. Emotions run high with FSBOs, and, unlike owners selling through an agent, they will be there as each buyers tours. They can hear every comment muttered under your breath and see every arched eyebrow.

If you really like this house, call and make an appointment for a second look. Write down the many questions that will have occurred to you since your first visit. You can use one of the computer printouts the real estate agent gave you about a property you have recently seen and draw up a similar one for the FSBO. That can help you ask the appropriate questions: size of the lot, date of construction, room dimensions, and so on.

On the second visit, poke around as much as you want, although you will probably want a house inspector at a later point to do a more thorough job (see Chapter 17). Still interested? Wait a day or two. That will heighten the seller's anticipation and make your offer sound well thought out.

A Few Final Words

You cannot pass over to a real estate agent, even a buyer's broker, the responsibility for finding you a perfect home and then making sure you become its owner. It is you who must watch out for your money and your happiness, and you who must make the right decisions each step of the way along the buying process. There is a lot of paperwork involved in a real estate transaction. Things move quickly. Mistakes can—and often are—made in one area of a property transfer or another, from stupendous blunders to trivial oversights. Your real estate agent can be an invaluable help to you, but it is up to you to continue working with your lender, house inspector, and everyone else involved, to get answers to your questions, to doublecheck documents and run figures through the calculator yet again. *You're* in charge here!

Tips to Remember

- Unless you engage a buyer's broker, remember that a real estate agent represents the seller of a house and her loyalty is with that individual.
- Choose a full-time real estate agent, one who is knowledgeable about the community that interests you and about financing packages.
- While being open with your real estate agent about other matters, never tell her the highest price you are willing to pay for a particular house. She is legally bound to tell the seller anything that will help get that individual the best price, including how high you are willing to go.

Nine
The Resale,
or "Used," House

A resale house is any dwelling that has been previously owned, even if that first owner is moving out after only six months. The resale house is more affordable, generally speaking, than brand-new homes, and can carry a price tag competitive with condos.

There are many advantages to buying a resale home. For one, the neighborhoods in which they are situated are "finished." There is not that stark, barren look of the new development. Houses of a certain vintage were sturdily constructed, with solid basements, thick plaster walls, and other materials that are not likely to be used these days because they are simply too expensive. And those old houses have architectural and design features that are also not incorporated in most of today's new houses, again because of cost.

There is, of course, a flip side to all the charm of oldness. Who needs an ancient heating system? Who wants the occasional design that seems dated rather than charmingly elderly? Or what about the expense of replacing old windows? Or adding proper insulation? And so on.

A study conducted a few years go by the Council of Better Business Bureaus showed two-thirds of homebuyers choose to buy a used home as opposed to a new one. You may be looking at a used home because you cannot afford the new house you prefer, or you may be aiming at the resale market because you like lived-in homes. Whatever your reasons, used homes, like used cars, have their own set of buyer guidelines.

Looking Around

The most important factor to consider in buying a home is its location.

In buying the most modest house in a higher-priced community, you can do very well indeed for yourself. You have an equally sound investment if your home is in the same price range as the ones around it. But if you buy what you consider a cute, cheap house in a bad neighborhood, you might just as well toss your potential investment out in a plastic trash bag.

While you are obviously going to be taken by the house you buy, it is important not to let yourself become interested in a home on any street that is fading fast or has already become off-limits to sensible investors. There is an exception here. There are neighborhoods in many cities and towns that are on the way *back* from decay and decline.

If you do not know where those enclaves are, you can discover them by reading the news articles in your real estate section, by going on house tours (most of their community associations sponsor one each year), by attending open houses and, of course, by driving by. Where you see three rundown houses and then one prettied up, perhaps with a window box, then another renovated one a few doors down, and an overall air of busyness and raking and exterior painting and neatly stacked bags of trash at the curb, you will know you have come across your area's newest revival neighborhood.

These communities offer some fine bargains for the novice buyer who feels priced out of just about every other neighborhood in his or her community. The only problem here is fixing up the houses, and many in revival areas need substantial rehabilitation. (There is more on fixer-upper opportunities and pitfalls in Chapter 10). If a house is priced surprisingly low it is for one of two reasons: the location is terrible, or at least noticeably beginning what looks like a steep decline, or the house requires a small fortune to bring it up to snuff. If the problem is location, that cannot be remedied. Move on to look at the next house on your list in a better neighborhood.

Real estate agents and everyone else in buying and selling homes agree that new homes are not necessarily better buys than older houses. What determines the value of each, specialists say, is its *location*.

Some more points to keep in mind as you look around:

• Stay away from a community with too many For Sale signs. Perhaps the only corporation in the area is relocating. Too much competition, with too many houses on the market, drives down the value of each property. Another thought: Do all of those home sellers know something you do not? Is there a master plan for the area that shows some new undesirable construction is moving in soon? If you can see no apparent reason for so many signs, it would be wise to head for town hall to see what's on the books, planning-wise, for that part of town.

• Avoid the house that has been overimproved for its block. You do not want the highest-priced house in the neighborhood.

• Look for a house that is traditional for its neighborhood. A California ultracontemporary home in a community of two-story Colonials could bring you problems when you want to sell if you cannot find a few souls who want that design plunked where it is.

• If you think you might be moving again in just a few

years, buy the most ordinary home you can find, one that can easily satisfy the greatest number of house seekers when you do decide to sell. This has long been a successful buying strategy for corporate transferees and military families.

• You will, of course, check into commuting time where you are looking, and schools, houses of worship, and nearby shopping.

• Ask the seller, or the real estate agent, about any extra fees that go along with the particular house that interests you. Besides real estate taxes, these can be costs for trash pickup or curbside recycling, and fees for mandatory membership in a community association.

• Be very sure that if you want to make any drastic changes to the appearance of the house, you will be able to do so according to that community's zoning laws. That could apply to a sunroom/greenhouse, constructing an extra bedroom or a garage, putting in an in-ground pool, and perhaps even a sturdy toolshed. Don't laugh at the latter. Some towns have made owners take down children's treehouses as zoning violations!

The Exterior of the Older Home

During your walking tour of homes you might buy, you ought to be asking yourself two questions: "Will I enjoy living here?" and "Will I be able to sell when I want to move and, I hope, with at least a small profit?"

Location is not the only factor that determines both satisfaction and investment appreciation. There are what are known as "features" in each home as well. Some are good, and some are a detriment to a house. How long you plan to stay in that home will also determine how you rate what you see. Do you expect to live there ten or more years? Then you will be looking for comfort. If you plan to move after five years or so, you are likely to be more interested in investment potential.

Every home is different, of course. Even resale houses in a development of seemingly look-alike homes have owners who have made their own improvements over the years. Here is a checklist to help you with what are, broadly speaking, the most wanted and most disliked features of most homes.

VIEWS AND LANDSCAPING

It is difficult to put a price tag on a view, although many sellers do just that. Sometimes a spectacular view will sell a house at a price higher than it would command on a more ordinary lot. Sometimes the house sells at the same price as those nearby without that unique feature. The view we are talking about here, incidentally, is the breathtaking distant horizon, not a look at a spectacular garden, or a stream at the end of the yard. The latter examples should not noticeably affect the asking price. Try not to fall in love with any view to the point where you overlook the house itself, settling for less inside than you wanted, or overlooking major flaws. Again, the investment potential of a view will always be questionable.

SITING

If you are a plant enthusiast, you will note fairly quickly where the house faces and its various other exposures. But there is more to siting than tracking the afternoon sun. Exposure can affect your heating and cooling bills. How many windows are there? Where is the morning light? Are there rooms that will remain dark most of the day? There are no absolute rights and wrongs with siting as far as investment potential goes. It is just a matter of taste.

CONSTRUCTION MATERIALS

Brick houses are the most desirable. Wood is fine, too, although somewhat less preferred in certain parts of the country because of the potential for termite damage. Vinyl or aluminum siding over a wood frame may or may not add to resale value, but will certainly save maintenance and money.

Stucco is attractive and widely used and accepted throughout the South and Southwest. In the North, however, stucco houses are often hard to sell because their unjointed surfaces are subject to cracking from the changeable weather. Stone and granite facades, on the other hand, do have expansion space and rarely cause problems.

GARAGES

The attached garage is best, both for your own use and as a plus when you are selling. Naturally, a two-car garage is better than one. Even if you are a one-auto family you will find the two-car garage valuable.

Garages located under the house are less desirable than ones attached to the side of the house. Some homeowners complain about drafts in rooms above below-house garages, and about higher heating costs. Ask yourself, too, whether you want to climb a flight of stairs to get to and from the garage.

Detached garages are unpopular in the North, in that few homeowners want to trudge through snow to get to their cars. In the South, however, detached is fine, and even carports are a plus.

PORCHES, DECKS AND PATIOS

All of these features rate high with househunters and are a good investment value. If the porch or patio is roofed and screened, this is even better.

WINDOWS

Self-insulating windows and sliding glass doors are considered positive features, although there are some homeowners who would argue that old-fashioned storm windows are better at keeping out the cold. If you are househunting in the North and find neither, you can expect to pay several thousand dollars for their installation. You probably *will* want one or the other, both for comfort, lower heating bills, and resale value. In the deep South, screened windows without storms are acceptable.

ENTRYWAYS

The front entrance should be attractive and well maintained for guests, and, of course, for resale value, in that it contributes to the overall first impression would-be buyers have of your home. However, *you* will probably find yourself using the back door far more often than the main entrance, so be sure to look at where the back door leads at the houses you walk through. The "ideal" back door—and you will find few of these—opens into a mud room, a back hallway, or cubicle where there is space to hang coats and remove wet boots. Another ideal setup is a laundry room adjacent to or combined with the back hall area, which saves toting dirty clothes, rugs, rags, and so on to a laundry area elsewhere in the house.

Back doors that open directly into a kitchen can be nuisance because of the traffic and clutter they create, but the kitchen is preferable to a family-room back door, especially if this room is access to a patio or other outside eating area.

Inside the House

Before going through houses you should have discussed at home what features you want, which ones would be nice to have but not necessary, and which you don't want to bother with at all. Here is what to look for, and beware of, as you visit homes for sale.

TRAFFIC PATTERN

A floor plan can make traffic in a home flow smoothly and seemingly effortlessly. Or it can puzzle, annoy, and inconvenience a family, making them wonder What *was* the architect thinking of? *He* should live here a week.

Questions to ask:

• Do you have to walk through one room to get to another? The kitchen is an acceptable walk-through room, but all others are a detriment to a sale. Be especially on the alert for floor plans where you must walk through one bedroom to get to another. These houses are very difficult to sell.

• How do you get from the kitchen to the backyard? If you have small children to watch, this will be especially important. But even other homebuyers will want the ease of going from a lawn chair to the refrigerator in an easy traffic pattern.

• Is there a powder room, and if so where is it? Consider entertaining and how guests will mix. Is the traffic flow easy from, say, the dining room to the living room?

• What is the traffic pattern for bringing groceries into the house? Remember the house with the garage downstairs. Will you want to climb steps with heavy bags?

KITCHENS

Most home shoppers want an eat-in kitchen. If you find one that is charming and sunny, you have a winner. Center islands are pluses, and gourmet cooks will look for a lot of unbroken counter space.

Abundant cabinet space is a feature usually mentioned in a sales pitch and is very desirable. So are broom closets, but many houses do not have them. Ask yourself where mops, buckets, brooms, and other cleaning agents will be stored. The garage? The laundry room?

Even if you are not at all interested in cooking, and microwave even breakfast, do not purchase a house that has an undesirable or nonworkable kitchen. It is, to most buyers, one of the most important rooms in a house. To many it is *the* most important. Always keep resale in mind.

BATHROOMS

Almost every buyer nowadays expects to find at least 1½ baths in a house, if not two full baths, or even 2½ baths. Many owners of older houses have had to remodel or even add to their homes to accommodate this expectation.

Walk-in shower stalls are preferred to shower-over-tub arrangements, but most folks want at least one bathtub in the house. Ceramic tile wins out over Formica, fiberglass, or vinyl paneling around the shower and on the walls.

Bathrooms with outside windows are preferable to those with vent fans, but buyers will take an extra bathroom with fans over none at all. Double sinks are a plus, as are full-wall mirrors behind the sink/vanity.

LAUNDRY FACILITIES

Is there a washer and dryer on the premises? Where are they located? A hookup in the basement is better than none at all, but many homeowners do not enjoy carrying laundry up and down stairs. Perhaps the two are in a separate room near the kitchen. This is everyone's first choice. Laundry facilities in an attached garage are satisfactory, although in some parts of the country homeowners do not like using the garage because of creepy-crawlies.

CLOSETS

There never seem to be enough of them. Large bedroom walk-in closets are a selling point and will make your life more comfortable, but look for other storage spaces. Is there a linen closet? A spot in the hall to hang hats and coats? A utility, or broom, closet? A closet near the back door, or at least an area where you can hang coats, can be invaluable.

BEDROOMS

Be sure to consider which family members will take which bedroom, and how existing furniture can be arranged (indeed, be sure it will fit) in the rooms. You should know, too, that attic rooms are preferable to newly created basement sleeping areas.

FAMILY ROOMS

Some say that family rooms are on their way out, replaced by the combination living/dining/kitchen area. Still, house shoppers with large families continue to look for a family room, and a large one at that. What *is* out of style is the basement rec room.

LIVING ROOMS

Almost all buyers want the living room to be formal and out of the path of day-to-day traffic, whether this room is small or sizable. A fireplace is a plus.

DINING ROOMS

Quite a few words have been written over the last few years on the theme Whither the dining room? Think about how you will use this room before you start walking through houses. Is a formal dining room a necessary part of your lifestyle? Or will you, as some seem to be doing these days, convert that room to a sort of second living room, but with a dining table? Some homeowners use this space for dining, certainly, but for family hanging-out purposes otherwise. Or will you convert this entire space to a family room? A dining room should be connected to the kitchen in some way, not separated by stairs or a hallway.

ATTICS

A true attic, with a real stairway leading up to that space, is a rarity these days, unless you are buying a house more than forty or so years old. If you find one of these upstairs nooks, you have excellent storage space or an extra bedroom if you choose. More commonly you will see pull-down stairs in a hallway that leads to this area, which will be just big enough to store some out-of-season clothing and the Christmas decorations.

BASEMENTS

Basements are high on a buyer's demand list in parts of the country where they are commonly used (primarily in the North). They should be dry and well lighted. Also very desirable is an exit to the outdoors. A basement with built-in shelving is a plus—more precious storage space.

In homes that do not have basements, a utility room for the furnace, water heater, air conditioner, and so on is usually located on a lower level, in a back corner of the house, or in a portion of an attached garage.

Community Associations

These are a fairly recent development on the housing scene. You are more likely to find these in new-home developments, of course, rather than older, established neighborhoods, but since your "resale" house might well be in a new community you should know about these groups.

What is it all about here in preserving property values. Covenants for these communities can say no satellite dishes, no backyard doghouses, no colored blinds, shades or curtains at the windows. They can carry requirements that color schemes be certain earthy or subdued tones, porches have awnings, all mailboxes be set back from the road a certain distance and look like all other mailboxes, and so on.

With some developments, membership in the owners association is mandatory, with others optional. Most charge an annual fee, if only as a fund for newsletters and the like, or perhaps to keep the entrance professionally landscaped.

There are pros and cons to buying into a neighborhood governed—and *governed* is the operative word here, in that some communities are run like mini-cities—by covenants. It is really your choice. But always, always ask if there is an owners association where you are looking, and request a copy of the covenants. Read every word to be sure you can live with the restrictions without feeling you have handed over some of your civil rights.

You might call your state homebuilders association to see if they have anything in writing for the consumer about community associations. They—and, of course, your lawyer—should be able to answer specific questions.

Inspections and Warranties

You are probably familiar with new-home warranties offered by developers. The seller is assuring the home-buyer that the house is, if not in excellent condition, at least covered for major repairs for twelve months, or however long the warranty runs. The only cost the buyer will pay during that time will be the price of the service call.

This warranty can be an excellent deal for you. For one thing, it saves you the cost of paying for your own inspection. It is true that having a plumber come in to replace a $2.39 widget at no cost to you will still cost you the $40 house call, but you could come up against far more costly repairs, where you stand to save many hundreds of dollars.

Some points to consider, however:

- Check exclusions. Warranties almost never cover structural elements such as roof repairs.
- Look to see if there are limits on preexisting conditions.
- Is there an extra charge for nonstandard items such as swimming pool equipment?

If no warranty is offered with the house that interests you, you can have your own inspection done, of course. You can purchase your own warranty, too. Better yet, ask if the seller will pay all or some of this cost. Chapter 17 covers house inspections in detail.

Tips to Remember

- The most important consideration in buying any home is its location.
- Before shopping, make a list of the features you *must* have in a home, those that you would *like* to have, and the ones that are unnecessary, and perhaps even undesirable.
- Try to avoid the largest and/or most expensive home on the block. Best bet: poorest-looking house on an otherwise solid block (if the house does not need too many repairs).
- In a like vein, shun the house that has been overimproved for its location.
- Most important rooms, resale-wise: kitchen and bathrooms.

TEN

Buying a Fixer-Upper and Paying for Repairs

The most important point you can carry away from this chapter is the admonition to avoid houses where *major* repairs are needed. That is, there are serious defects in the foundation, high-priced repairs needed to the working systems, or a major reshuffling of rooms necessary to create a workable traffic pattern. All of this work is expensive, and does not add to the market value of the house. When you sell, a buyer will *expect* that your home will have workable plumbing and heating, adequate wiring, workable room layouts, and so on. A new roof comes under the heading of a major improvement, this *can* add to value because it improves the appearance of the home.

If you have the ability to virtually build a house yourself, or if you have family engaged in one phase or another of the construction trades, these cautionary words might not apply. Broadly speaking, however, truly rundown houses are just too far gone for the novice homebuyer to attempt to salvage.

There are two exceptions to that caveat. One is the tumbledown house purchased by a *professional* renovator who is buying, renovating, and selling for profit.

The second fixer-upper who could profit in all areas from buying the most distressed property possible could be the one going into a new restoration area, where there are dilapidated houses that with enough care (and funds) can eventually be worth *a lot* of money.

What you as a first-time buyer ought to look at seriously

are houses that need painting, landscaping, minor or medium-size repairs, carpeting, and other cosmetic improvements. Upgrading the kitchen and bathrooms can also be profitable when it comes to resale, and so will adding a second bathroom. These houses look untended and slightly shabby. They do not look like bombed-out shells.

You will have to use your own judgment in determining how much fixing up you will be able to undertake, both emotionally and financially. There are a number of points to keep in mind while shopping for the least expensive, yet potentially most salvageable and profitable fixer-upper.

• Prices for shabby properties might be almost as high where you are as prices for houses in better condition. It is important not to overpay for *any* house, but particularly important that you not spend all of your money on a house that needs still more money—and big bucks, at that—to make it livable.

• Remember location, of course. A rundown house in a solid or even pretty darn attractive neighborhood can be a good investment. Alas, too many of those dwellings are in equally rundown blocks, where no amount of renovating can increase their value. For a guide to determining if what appears to you to be a marginal enclave is on the skids, or is being restored and coming back, see Chapter 9.

• If the fixer-upper you are considering has been on the market for a long time, ask yourself why. It may be all the work it needs, but it could be for other reasons. Let's say it's very dark. That defect could be remedied by installing a skylight, an idea that might not have occurred to other house shoppers. Be creative as you go through these homes. Knowing how to fix flaws that might have turned off other buyers to a basically sound property could bring you an excellent deal. Or the seller might just be asking a too-high price.

• As you walk through fixer-uppers, make notes on repairs needed (a house inspector will do a more thorough job later, of course). Then take out your calculator when you return home and figure roughly how much you will need in repair costs. If you cannot estimate costs of some malfunction or other, at least list the problem, with a repair figure to be filled in later. Seeing a sizable list of wrongs could well turn you off to buying a particular property.

• Speaking of work, consider who will do the repairs in the house you buy. It is most cost effective if the owners do most of the work themselves. Labor costs are high, and in the ideal situation the professionals are called on only for highly specialized areas such as electrical work, plumbing and heating, and the like. You should be willing to do as much as possible of the other jobs, with a little help from the folks at the local home decorating center.

• Look into local zoning restrictions when you find a house that interests you. Be sure that you can renovate the way you want, particularly if you want to add an extension to the house. Perhaps you will not be permitted to do so, or you will require a variance. Are you sure you can win one? Do you want to go to that much trouble?

• Is the renovation work going to be so drastic, or so messy, that you will be unable to live in the house until most of the work is complete? If so, where *will* you live? Can you afford to carry a mortgage payment, to rent where you are now, and perhaps to make a home repair loan each month?

If you feel you can live there while work is in progress, try to organize yourselves to settle in for the long haul. Be certain your family, and your marriage, can stand the strain of the always present odor of sawdust and paint, the constant walking around ladders and planks of wood and the sense that life, even away from the house, is always going to be messy, dirty, and incomplete.

• How much time are you going to be able to devote to a renovation project with your work schedule? Do you travel in your job? Do you put in fourteen-hour days? Is your spouse equally busy in a demanding career? Consider all of this in determining just how grand a rehab project you can undertake. If you say "Well, we'll work on the house weekends," you will be surprised at how soon you begin to tire of that weekend agenda. It ceases being fun and challenging and even romantic after, say, three months. Six months, tops.

• Buying a house in a designated historic district brings its own special concerns. Here you may be restricted from making the types of changes you envision to the property that interests you. Exterior alternations will in all likelihood have to be approved by a local commission. Exterior surfacing and paint colors might be regulated. You will almost certainly be allowed to do anything you want *inside* the house, although extensions, even knocking out a flat window to create a bay, will also call for district approval.

Learn all you can about the district that interests you before you make an offer on any property inside its boundaries. Homes in these enclaves usually retain their value and cachet because of the uniform appearance of the neighborhoods. Still, some househunters do not like the restrictions or curbs to their own artistic expressions.

• A house inspection makes good sense in buying any resale home. In putting down your life savings on a house that could be a problematical investment it is vital. Chapter 17 covers the subject of house inspections.

What Should You Pay for a Fixer-Upper?

When considering what to bid, take the market value of the house (Chapter 18 explains how to determine this), deduct what you think repairs will cost, add a little extra in the event you lowballed the repairs figure, and you should come up with a fair offer. Another formula. How much would this house be worth if it were in top-grade condition? Let's say the asking price is $95,000. But it could bring $110,000 with some improvements. You should buy at 20 to 30 percent below what the house would cost if it were not a fixer-upper. So, 20 percent of $110,000 is $22,000. You might consider an offer of $88,000, or even lower, to start (Chapter 18 also goes into negotiating over price).

In the contract you should state "subject to the buyer obtaining a satisfactory inspection report and satisfactory repair bids within 10 business days." The inspection phrase is standard these days; the repair bids phrase should be incorporated in fixer-upper bids. If you do not approve of the reports and recommendations you receive from the house inspector and from the repair people you call in for estimates, you can cancel the agreement to purchase and have your earnest money deposit refunded.

Financing the Fixes

If you are successful in winning a price break for your handyman's special because of its condition, you may still fall short financially of the money you need to make repairs.

With the federal government's 203(k) program, you can

combine a mortgage and home improvement loan in one package. This could be one source of funding. Now on to some others.

• There is a relatively new financing service called the Community Home Improvement Mortgage Loan program, but it does have income limits for borrowers. Introduced by Fannie Mae and GE Capital Mortgage Insurance Corporation, the program lets buyers finance both the purchase of a home and its renovation in a single mortgage.

You are eligible for these loans if you earn less than 115 percent of your area's median family income. In some higher-cost areas, the program may be extended to families earning less than 140 percent of the median, or even a little more. The loans can cover up to 95 percent of purchase and repair costs *combined*.

This program is so far available only in several major cities. To learn more, call GE Capital Mortgage at 1-800-876-4343, or write FNMA Public Information Office, CHIML, 3900 Wisconsin Avenue NW, Washington, D.C. 20016-2899.

• You should get out the phone book, too, and call your regional office of the U.S. Department of Housing and Urban Development (HUD), which will be listed under federal government offices. Ask the HUD representative what regional and local home improvement loan programs [other than 203(k)] are available where you are and whether you are qualified to borrow. These can run from national FHA, VA and FmHA programs to strictly local home improvement programs, where money is offered almost on a block-by-block basis, depending on where sprucing up is needed in that community. All of these programs, where you can find them and where you qualify, are likely to offer terms better than you will find at local lending institutions.

• In the area of help from the government, but from the state and not federal branch, you can call your Governor's Office for the name and number of your state Housing Finance Agency or Mortgage Finance Agency—the office that offers homes to first-time buyers at very attractive borrowing terms—to see how they can help with fixer-upper expenses. There may be income ceilings for qualifiers, however.

• You can see what your contractor has to offer in the way of a loan. They sometimes offer financing, on terms that can be better or worse than you would find elsewhere, so continue to shop even after you get a contractor's quote on rates. On the debit side, you give up important leverage when you finance through a contractor. Since the loan is usually paid to the contractor by the lending institution, you lose some power to withhold payment if you are not satisfied with the job.

• Consider your credit union, if you belong to one, which is always a good source of financing at attractive terms.

• Finally, you can apply for an unsecured home improvement loan with your local bank or savings and loan association. Terms and amounts that can be borrowed vary from one lender to another, but generally you can expect to be able to borrow as much as $20,000, for five or ten years, at a fairly high interest rate, usually a point or two above the current rate.

With this type of loan you do not offer your house or other assets as collateral. You are judged for eligibility on income, job security, good credit history—all of the requirements for any loan or mortgage. The lender may well want to see three written estimates for the work you want done with these loans.

As you can see, you have a variety of choices here. You *can* secure rehab money for your diamond in the rough. However, if buying a house in itself is going to be an uphill struggle for you, carrying that mortgage payment plus a home improvement loan could make the endeavor impossible. Be careful you do not take on more financing than you can afford, and more house work than you can reasonably be expected to do. But if you do manage to find a nicely priced fixer-upper, and lock into an improvement loan with excellent terms, you could have a home that will appreciate in value quite nicely.

Tips to Remember

- Be very sure the fixer-upper you want is worth salvaging! A house inspector can help you calculate repair costs.
- The best houses look shabby, need painting, landscaping, minor or medium-size repairs, and perhaps kitchen and/or bathroom upgrading. Avoid those where major work is called for.
- To save money, do as much of the work yourself as you can.
- You need to be financially and emotionally able to undertake a rehabilitation project, *and* have the time to devote to it.
- You will also need to consider whether you can carry a monthly mortgage payment and perhaps a sizable home improvement loan.

ELEVEN

Maybe You Can Swing a New-Development Home

Brand-new houses and tight budgets do not seem to belong in the same sentence, but let's see. The theme of this book, after all, is to consider *everything*.

New houses are more expensive than resale homes, all things being equal. Quite a few thousand dollars more expensive, in fact, and the dollar spread between the two rises every year. However, it might be possible for you to purchase a new house in a development. We are talking about single-family homes here. More than likely you *can* find affordable new condominiums and townhomes in your price range.

How to Find the New Affordables

You can start by looking beyond the city limits, and most likely beyond the suburbs. You will get a better deal on homes way, way out, where the developer has not paid astronomical rates for land. Where such homes are situated is vitally important. Part of the attraction of the developments you will be investigating will be their reasonable price, and that should bring in buyers and future buyers. But you want a reasonable number of existing services there now. Are there schools, stores, houses of worship and recreational amenities, or will you truly be trailblazers?

Keep in mind that it is not the dream house, all new and shiny, but the total picture that makes for a successful home purchase. Look at your lifestyle to see if you might be sacrificing too much just for a sparkling new house.

Another suggestion for finding affordables: Look for the innovative builders in your area who specialize in *quality* medium-cost construction. Hovnanian Enterprises, for example, is a company that has made homeowners of thousands of first-timers in Florida, New Jersey, and most recently with developments in North Carolina and Pennyslvania.

Hovnanian offers solid construction in an attractive community, with homes that are more or less free of frills (unless buyers choose to pay more for extras). Each is on a small, nicely landscaped lot. The complexes are well maintained and resale is never a problem.

When looking at new construction, beware, just as you would in a traditional neighborhood, of the largest, flashiest house. Look instead at the midpriced or lower-end models. The value of these homes will be pulled up by the splashier ones around them. The only exception would be a community that stresses recreational amenities, where being right on the golf course, say, or on the lake, would be the top-of-the-line location. Pick the home with the best view of what the community has to offer.

Owners Associations

Many new-home communities come with formal associations to which members must belong and perhaps pay dues. There can be many, many restrictions as to lifestyle and home decorating attached to life in communities with associations, albeit many pluses. There is a more complete discussion of this relatively new factor in single-family home communities in Chapter 9.

Negotiating to Sweeten the Deal

Developers do not usually like to lower sales prices because this will cut the appraised value of future home sales in a particular development. However, the state of the economy, both national and local; the developer's finances; and other factors could make him quite amenable to "talking."

The trick here is to keep cool. As with other types of negotiating, it is not a good idea to seem too excited about what someone is trying to sell you. Oooh and aaah too much and the builder or the on-site sales agent is going to think "This one is hooked," and there go your bargaining chips.

When a community is essentially finished and running smoothly, a developer may well want to "close out" that complex as quickly as he can. If there are two or three houses that remain stubbornly unsold, he might lower their price. Occasionally the model home might be sold that way, although it could also be sold early, with the deal not officially consummated until the developer is prepared to close down sales. The developer who has *many* unsold homes is also likely to be amenable to a little negotiating. It costs money to carry empty houses.

In the off season for homebuying, generally October through January or February, when developers are drumming their fingers on desk tops in sales offices, you will also look *very* welcome, and all of the stops might be pulled out to keep you from looking elsewhere. What is more likely than a price cut is negotiating with the developer over what will be included in a sales price that stays firm. All the little extras can add up, and it is up to you to ask for them. Perhaps a house is selling for $97,000, and you know you are going to spend another $3,000 for decorating features you want. If you get that $3,000 from the developer in the form of extras, that is $3,000 that can stay in your savings account.

Be careful, though, with frills. If the builder tells you, "I'll cut the price by $5,000 for you, or give you $5,000 in credit that you can use to buy the things you want from our design center," take the price cut. There is usually quite a markup on developers' upgrades.

Analyze all concessions offered you. Some may well be a value, whereas others don't stand up to a pocket calculator. Perhaps you can secure a commitment from the developer to pay your first year's real estate taxes, your moving expenses, or part of the closing costs.

Buying a House
Before It's Built

Buying a home before it is constructed carries its own set of caveats—and its own potential price shavings. Again, as you read the real estate section of the local paper, you will often see advertisements with headlines like these: "Preconstruction Prices Through September 15"; "Preconstruction Prices for Phase II of Pheasant Run;" "Special Preview Offer." What does all of this mean? Is it good for you, or just another sales come-on?

Obviously, a preconstruction price is the first place at which a new development house is offered. That is when Pheasant Run is probably a sea of mud. Developers concede they underprice a little at the beginning to get the ball rolling. How much can you save? Houses sold when the development is complete can be 20 to 30 percent more than the price of preconstruction homes!

Assuming you can wait for your home to be built, and that the builder is reputable, this can be a very good deal for you. The money you are now putting aside for the remainder of the downpayment you will need could be earning interest for you while you are waiting for the builder to finish.

One problem might be some uncertainty about when you will actually have the house. Sometimes there are construction delays and delivery snags—and if you need to get into your new home *now*, you can become a nervous wreck—but you *will* have a lower price that is locked in. How much lower depends on the developer, but you could save 10 to 15 percent on homes offered in a preconstruction phase versus prices asked for comparable existing models elsewhere. Buying early also gives you a choice of location; you do not have to take what's left.

Some important points to keep in mind here:

• Know your builder. It is best to go with someone who has done similar construction and has completed such jobs. Look for a single-family developer who has completed other single-family projects, not someone with a record of shopping center construction who is now dipping into the residential arena. Drive around his other projects, even if you have to head thirty miles out of your way some Sunday afternoon. Talk to those homeowners if you can, too, and ask them if they are satisfied with their houses. If this is the builder's first job, you cannot know if he will finish. What if he disappears with your deposit—and leaves the community awash in unpaved roads, semi-built homes and unlandscaped yards? Alas, this has been known to happen.

• If you're one of the early buyers in a new-home

community, will you be able to accept living virtually alone until more people move in? Maybe you will be the first buyer, or perhaps the fifth. In any event, you are likely to be living in a pretty unfinished state for some time. What about the safety factor? Can children play in the area? Can you drive around the development and access roads in bad weather? Will you mind the constant noise of construction? Just how primitive will life be as a pioneer settler?

• You will want to add a paragraph to your contract stating that there will be no design changes or switches in any materials used on your house without your written approval. To make sure your house is the same as the model, get a copy of the blueprints and specifications and have them become a part of the contract.

• You might want to have an architect review all of the material in your contract, including blueprints and specs, of course, to be sure there are no hidden design problems or serious faults, such as with the foundation. Naturally you will not hire the developer's architect or anyone he suggests.

• Once a contract is signed, the sales figure— preconstruction or not—is usually protected no matter how many times a developer later raises the prices of homes.

• Concerned about delivery delay? You can ask for a clause in the contract requiring the builder to notify you two months in advance of completion date, a factor that will help establish a time frame for your leaving where you are living now.

• If you are buying a small home and are already considering expanding it, be sure that you can do so following local regulations, and even according to convenants of the new-home community.

Downpayment and Financing
Help from the Developer

In some new-home communities the developer will do all he can to help you buy, including shaving downpayment requirements to as low as 5 percent, and offering financing at attractive rates. He is able to do this through his relationship with the bank or other lender who is handling the financing for the project.

By all means jot down all of the information he provides about mortgage loans and interest rates. But then do some comparison shopping. His rate might not be the best. It *is* likely to be short-term. Discount financing programs are not likely to last longer than, say, three years. After that, they convert to market rates. So bring out the calculator again to determine how much you can save with what he offers.

Checking Out the Place
Before You Move In

There will be an initial walk-through of your new home, where you have a chance to assure yourself that the builder has completed the job to your satisfaction. Anything that has not been completed, or is not up to standard, you should jot down on what is known as a punch list. Do not be so taken with how marvelous the house looks that you neglect to check every little detail. This is your chance to have anything set to rights. Ask the builder to fix all of the problems on your punch list before the closing. Then make a final inspection to see that indeed all of these problems have been solved.

Sometimes the builder may contest your complaint. If a

problem remains unresolved as closing nears, you can defer the closing until all of the questionable points have been cleared up. If the builder offers you cash instead of repairs, decline and ask for the repairs. They could cost more than the cash allowance he will make to you.

Be sure that you take both walk-throughs when you have time to spare. This is not something you want to rush through. You will have to live with any unreported faults, or pay for having them corrected.

Remember *you* hold all the cards before the closing. If ever there is a time to get the corrections you want, this is it. Your leverage drops way down after you take title to the house.

What to check? What is on the punch list and anything that it did not cover. Check everything from the attic for ventilation to the stairs for creaks to the walls to be sure they are plumb. If you have any doubt about your ability to take such a microscopic look at a new house, you might want to engage a house inspector to go along with you. There is more about inspections in Chapter 17.

Warranties

You could be offered a builder's warranty against problems with your new house, which is a one-year protection plan not backed by an independent warrantor. Like most warranties, these plans cover the house against structural defects and malfunctions of the working systems. But if your builder has gone under, or is no longer on the scene for one reason or another, you will be out of luck and your chances of being reimbursed for repairs you have made will be practically nonexistent.

However, if your house is covered by an *insured* warranty, you are, shall we say, home clear. These plans are usually ten-year policies written by an independent warrantor, such as Home Owners Warranty (HOW). If anything goes awry with your builder, your claim, if considered a legitimate one, will be honored by these warrantors.

Try to secure both from your developer, although, of course, you will have this one-year protection automatically. You can use his payment of the insured policy premium as a negotiating tool. In the event he firmly refuses, you ought to purchase a policy on your own. A few hundred dollars is little to pay to ensure the proper functioning of an investment of many, many times that figure.

Tips to Remember

- You can negotiate—over price and extras—in a new-home community the same way you would in buying a resale house. In fact, bargain as much as you can, especially in a slow market.
- Besides location, the reputation of the developer is vital to a successful new-home community.
- Ask the developer for an *insured* warranty. If he says no, purchase such a policy on your own.

TWELVE
Why Not
Become a Landlord?

One of the very best ways you can ease yourself into a home of your own is by purchasing a house that has rental space. What can make this even more appealing is that mortgage lenders will often take rent into account when calculating whether you are mortgage-worthy, which can push you into the category of approved.

The rent will also, of course, pay a good deal of your housing expenses—perhaps your entire mortgage payment. Maybe even mortgage and real estate taxes. This all depends, of course, on the going rents in the area you have chosen, and how much you pay for the house.

Just think how you would feel knowing there is another $450 or $600 coming in each month? Without your having to moonlight! Without, sometimes for many, many months, having to do much at all in the way of maintenance or repairs.

Having an apartment to rent can be a particular relief for those in precarious professions—the self-employed, for example, and those whose positions are always in danger of cutback or subject to the vagaries of the marketplace. No matter what happens at your workplace, the rent check will be slipped under your door each month. There will be some money coming in—perhaps along with unemployment checks—to keep you going while you look for other work.

There is more good news. The repairs and new installations you make to that rental unit are tax deductible. The apartment's share of your repairs to the house as a whole—a new roof, for example—are also deductible. So, if you live on two floors of the house and the tenants on one, one-third of the price of the roof can be deducted. Check with your accountant for the latest on this and on depreciation allowances.

On the Other Hand

Of course there is a flip side, just as there is a flip side to owning a house instead of renting. There *will* be people—strangers—stomping around above you or below you. If you have lived in an apartment building, or a house converted to two or more apartment units, this should not bother you. Others may find it disquieting—at first. Soon it becomes an everyday part of your life.

Private homes converted to two or three separate living units, which is what you will be seeking, do not usually appreciate as quickly in market value as single-family houses. They can also take somewhat longer to sell when you are ready to move on. This should not be too much of a problem, however, in that real estate is not a liquid investment and selling even the most desirable house in one day will not bring you instant cash.

What Being a Landlord Entails

You will have to be as responsible owning a two-family house as those who run large apartment complexes are supposed to be. If something is broken, you must fix it, and promptly. *You* can put up with a roof that leaks with each rainfall because money is too tight for a roofer right now. But if the *tenants* are on the top floor, you will have to come up with the cash for repairs somehow. It is not just an ethical point. Tenants are entitled by law to premises that are habitable, and any serious lack of repairs on your part, where those renters are without heat, light, or water, or where it is raining down on them from a damaged roof, can result in their heading for the local landlord/tenant enforcement agency and/or withholding rent. A mess.

Smaller repairs are a different story. You do not have to drop everything to mend systems or appliances that are not basic and do not contribute to making an apartment fit for habitation. Some repairs you can just add to your list and get around to within a reasonable length of time. The tenants will let you know eventually what they consider reasonable.

If rent control is an ordinance where you live, you will have to adhere to these regulations. They set by law when you can raise rents and how often. You may have to register your house with the local regulating agency.

This is important: If you find a house you like, you have the option of having the sales contract state you want that house delivered vacant, which means the seller will have to give the tenant notice to move. Or you can, if you choose, allow that tenant to stay when you become owner.

Be sure here that the tenant is paying an adequate rent and has been a responsible renter. The former is easy to find out by asking the seller for rent receipts. The latter is more difficult. An eager seller may praise Mr. Thirdfloor to the skies. You could also be entering the ticklish area of wanting the house vacant, which means the seller will have to tell 71-year-old Mr. Thirdfloor that he will have to move from his rent-controlled $135 a month flat. Or, perhaps in your state, or according to local laws, senior citizens are protected from having to move in this situation. You will have to continue having Mr. Thirdfloor as your tenant, and must be very careful that his $135 a month does not cause you financial hardship because you had counted on $400 a month coming in from that apartment.

Generally, those who own and live in buildings (houses) with three residential units or less are exempt from many local regulations that govern landlords of larger properties. Your state Department of Community Affairs or your local property owners association, or even tenant association, can fill you in on your rights and responsibilities here. Make the acquaintance of these folks before you start househunting for a two-family property, so that you do not sign on a dotted line and *then* learn your restrictions.

Finding the Right House

This is extremely important because your ability to rent the apartment in your house will depend on several factors. Is the house convenient to the downtown, suburban office park? Or to a college or university? Where will the tenants—and you—park your cars? Does the house you are looking at need so much work that paying for repairs through a home-improvement loan will cancel out a year or two of rent coming in? This is all right if you can do without profits for that length of time.

Most areas of the country are facing or are already in the midst of a shortage of rental housing. Developers over the last several years have steered clear of new rental construction, preferring condominiums and townhomes. Also, more renters are staying in apartments these days because they cannot afford to buy. Still, while this shortage is pronounced nationwide, it might not be true where you live.

You need also to beware of buying this type of property if apartments in houses are a rarity where you are because there are dozens of new rental complexes in your town, and most folks gravitate to the new. You will be competing here with waste disposals, bathroom exhaust fans, built-in microwaves, and the latest refrigerator models. Not to mention the pool, tennis courts, and clubhouse you almost certainly do not have! You will have a hard time finding tenants unless you are offering rents substantially lower than those of the glossier complexes.

Ask yourself when looking at any two-family house: Who is my likely tenant? Will I have enough to offer them with this house? Nose around a little too during this thinking stage. Read real estate *articles* in your local papers, not just the advertisements. What is the rental situation like?

It is better if the house you buy has a separate entrance for tenants so they do not have to walk through any part of your apartment. The only way you can discard that generally applicable standard is if you are buying in a college town (where houses are probably too expensive for the first-timer buying on a shoestring anyway) or in a downtown, "hot" back-to-the-city market, where everyone, especially young singles, is interested in living.

The tenant's unit does not have to be as nice as yours, of course, but in looking through houses, be sure it is nice enough to bring in the rent you want. Will it need much charming up? Can *you* do it, or will you have to farm out the work at high labor costs?

It is interesting what some low-cost improvements can do to a rather boring floor-through apartment in an ordinary-looking house. Many a professional renovator has made a bundle by adding touches that resulted in higher rents than the average (and a nice high sales price when it was time to move on).

When looking at the tenant's unit, consider adding new doors (doors only) to the kitchen cabinets; add a mantelpiece in the living room, even if there is no chance for a fireplace (the opening can be filled with a basket of flowers, or artificial flames if the tenant chooses). Keep wallpaper very neutral, however, and paint even more so. White is preferred throughout.

You might have the floors sanded if they are hardwood, which is the flooring of choice these days over wall-to-wall carpeting. If the house is an old one, a medallion ceiling in at least one of the rooms can be installed at low cost. Try, too, for attractive ceiling lights. Ceiling fans add an interesting touch, besides being practical and energy saving. A skylight can brighten up a dreary hallway, or too-dark bathroom. All of these expenses should be included in your doodling as you walk through houses and estimate repair and fixup costs.

Open for Business

Once you have closed on your two-family property you probably will not waste time fixing up the apartment and looking for a tenant. In fact, most homebuyers in your situation work on the tenant's unit before their own, to get that rental money coming in as quickly as possible.

How do you calculate the rent? You can check the classified advertisements in your local papers for an idea of what other owners are charging for similar apartments. But remember, there are all sorts of variables to consider here. Apartment A may not be as fancy as yours, but it is two blocks from the grammar school and you are eight blocks away—and another six from the bus stop for the ride into the city.

You can talk to some local real estate agents about rents

in your area. Some have index cards showing listings of apartments for rent, with pictures and the rents being asked, in their windows. You are under no obligation to any real estate agency you query. Most help as a service because they hope to secure your rental unit as their listing, and, in the future, your house, when you decide to sell. It pays them to be nice. Renting is often a sideline to their more profitable business, which is selling.

If you do give a real estate agent your listing, he or she will find you a tenant, usually at no fee. *Be sure that the agent checks references.* Some are in a hurry to conclude a deal and do not bother.

If you run an advertisement yourself asking for a tenant (another tax deductible expense), list only your telephone number, not your name and not the address of the property. Do put in the rent you are asking, along with a brief description of the apartment. It is a pain in the neck for would-be tenants not to know the rent, and you will just be bothered by phone calls from the curious if you leave it out.

Even in rent-controlled communities you can set your own initial rent in a house where you have a new apartment to offer. The limits come in after that, when you must conform to regulations about the percentage of each increase and when you can ask for raises. So be sure your initial rent is as high as you can reasonably expect to get, since this figure is not going to rise substantially while those first tenants are in residence. Even when they move out, if you are in a rent-controlled community, you can be limited in the increase you can charge the next tenants.

Be sure that you also take into account what that rent will cover. Will the tenants pay their own utilities? This generally means water and gas or electric. What about heat? Is the house metered for two separate units, or are you all on a master system? If you will have to pay some or all of these costs yourself, the rent should reflect this.

The Tenant Search

Screening tenants is not an aspect of landlording you will enjoy, although it does get easier in time. It is best to work up a form for everyone to fill out with the name, address, phone number and number of years they have been living there; previous landlords; employer and number of years on the job (the self-employed should supply tax returns for the previous two years).

Get a credit check if you can from a local reporting bureau, or ask the prospect to supply one. If you work through a real estate agent, this office should be able to secure a credit report.

Verify all information supplied, even if doing so requires many phone calls. Checking references will not necessarily tell you all you want to know, however. Your applicant's current landlord may give a glowing reference because he is *dying* to get rid of a problem tenant. Similarly, what applicant is going to list anyone as a personal reference who will have something bad to say? Try earlier landlords, who have nothing to lose by being truthful.

Saying "no pets" may be a hasty decision. Because some apartment complexes ban them, and many homeowners will not allow them in their rental units, you stand to have a larger pool of applicants if you say okay. Try, if you can in your community, to secure a pet fee of an extra $100 over your security deposit, or ask for a month and a half's security. You will probably have to spend some money cleaning up after the tenants and pet leave, and you cannot count on using their security money because they often do not pay the last month's rent, letting the security deposit cover it.

You can pick up a standard apartment lease from your local stationery store. Fill in all of the blanks, and add your own special riders. They are written by owners' groups, so they are slanted in your favor. Spell out everything, down to who tends the lawn.

If the idea of rolling up your sleeves and working for your house even after you have moved in does not bother you because you see the benefits of rent coming in, then you *can* successfully wear the hat of landlord.

Tips to Remember

- Be sure that you can carry the responsibilities and obligation of landlord before you look seriously at two-family houses.
- Acquaint yourself with local rental regulations as soon as you decide to buy this type of housing.
- Rents must be set at what the market will bear in your community, not at how much *you* need each month to cover expenses.
- Make any needed repairs in the house to the tenant's unit first, to get rent coming in.
- Check prospective tenants' references carefully.

THIRTEEN
Condos, Co-Ops, Townhomes, and Patio Homes

If you elect to purchase one of these home styles, you could save $10–30,000—or more—over the price of a single-family house comprising the same space. Do you need three bedrooms? This is no problem. Do you want a two-car garage? Very possible. You can also frequently enjoy a swimming pool, tennis courts, fitness center, and clubhouse right on the grounds of your complex.

Overall, as a first-time buyer, you will probably be able to live in a better location with a condo than you would if you purchased a traditional, resale single-family home. This is because there are so many others along with you sharing the expense for the landscaping and amenities you enjoy. There are some serious cautions that go with a condo purchase, but in the main, condos have made homeowners out of millions of entry-level househunters, many of whom, if it were not for that apartment style, would still be renting.

First, some terms of enlightenment. Townhomes are two-story attached units that feature the sleeping quarters upstairs. They are usually run in a joint-ownership style, the way the condo is, with residents joining an owners association and paying a monthly maintenance fee to this entity.

Patio homes are just the opposite of townhomes. They are one-floor units with a patio or deck in the rear. But here, unlike the condo, owners generally buy their own unit, plus the land under and around it (their front and back yard). They also own an equal interest in any common areas. Membership in the owners association can cover yard care, if the members have so elected. Or that, too, can be left to each owner. Fees then would cover only prorated common area expenses.

Cooperatives are a form of legal ownership and not an architectural style. In a co-op, tenants own their building by purchasing shares in it and forming a corporation to pay maintenance and repairs. There is more about co-ops later in this chapter.

The most popular of apartment ownership styles is, of course, condominiums, so virtually all of this chapter will concern itself with buying and living in a condo unit. If, however, you prefer townhomes or patio homes, by all means continue reading these pages. The advice here—on choosing a location, and plowing through bylaws and the like—will apply to you too.

Why So Popular?

For the twenty-five or so years of its growth in this country, the condominium has been considered *the* starter home for the first-time home buyer. Indeed, retirees and first-timers form the principal makeup of many complexes. For retirees, the attraction is smaller, more manageable living space, the amenities, and, to a lesser extent, lower costs than house maintenance. To the first-timer, the appeal is almost always cost. Next comes minimal upkeep. Many first-time buyers say that they are busy with careers and do not want to spend their little free time on house repairs. They want fun, and if a condo community comes with a pool, tennis courts, and clubhouse, so much the better.

The condo can be an excellent starter home, freeing its owner at least from the "rent check down the drain" style of life. It can be a reasonably sound investment, too, allowing a unit owner to trade up later to a house if he or she chooses, or perhaps a fancier condo complex. However, if chosen for the wrong reasons or without sufficient thought, it can also be a very unsatisfactory style of living—and impossible when it comes time to sell and there are 2,500 condo units in eight condo complexes within three square miles!

What a Condo Is and How It Works

Condos actually date back to ancient Rome, and have been in existence in Europe far longer than they have here.

It is not a building style that determines a condo, but the legal system of ownership. A condominium complex, however it is laid out, is a shared-ownership community. residents own their own apartment, or "unit," and they own a proportional share of what is known as the common areas. These are such areas as the driveway leading to the complex, with its landscaping; the carports or garages, if they exist; all of the land outside each unit, including the bushes just under each window. If there are recreational amenities, these, too, are held jointly by owners.

You purchase a condo the same way you would any house. That is, you can work with a real estate agent, or perhaps drive around the community you like and see a sign on the lawn (its size could have been regulated by the community association) advertising a unit for sale by its owner. You apply for a mortgage the same way you would for a new or resale house. The negotiating over price, the closing—all of the steps toward ownership follow the lines of any property transaction.

Your mortgage interest is tax deductible, and so are the real estate taxes for your unit. You are also allowed a tax deduction for your share of real estate taxes on the common areas. You will know that amount from a statement sent to you by the owners' association. The monthly maintenance fee *cannot* be deducted.

There is more to living in a condo than knowing the legal workings, however. If you are moving from an apartment building, you will probably pick up the condo way of life quite easily. If you have been living on a military base, or on a college campus, you, too, will quickly grasp what's what in the condo lifestyle. But if you are buying a condo after living in a private home, you will need a bit of orientation. As you read the next several pages, you may feel quite accepting of the restrictions and privileges of condo life. Or you might mutter "Nope, not for me" and flip over to the next possibility. It is not for everyone.

For one thing, every new condo buyer must join the association that "runs" the community. Let's call the complex that interests you The Brierwood. You will be expected to join the Brierwood Community Association, which represents the 250-unit complex and its owners, and is run by a volunteer board of directors elected from among residents. Your dues are, say, $130 a month. This fee covers your share of the community's real estate taxes, insurance on the common areas, the cost of landscaping, pool maintenance, perhaps monthly extermination calls on each unit, and, one hopes, a little extra that goes into a fund to cover upcoming expenses in the complex. Such expenses might be replacing a section of roofing over two or three units, or perhaps buying play equipment for a patch of land within the community that residents voted for use as a playground.

Maintenance fees will vary according to the size of the complex and the number of auxiliary features, buildings, or amenities that form the total expense for running the community. Naturally, the fancier a place looks, the more it costs to run and the more you will have to pay each month to keep it going.

The money-collecting, bill-paying, and purchasing could be handled by the board of directors, or it might be under the jurisdiction of a local property management company the owners association has hired. If there is such a company, its fee has also been added into the monthly maintenance charge for all residents.

The association holds an annual meeting, which you can attend or not, and perhaps a few other sessions throughout the year. There might be a regularly published newsletter.

You do not live alone in a condo. You are one of a group, and that calls for team spirit. You have to consider your neighbors in this housing style more than you would in any other, except the cooperative, which is even more restrictive.

BYLAWS; CONDITIONS, COVENANTS, AND RESTRICTIONS; AND RULES AND REGULATIONS

There is a lot in writing to plow through when purchasing a condo. You can be a loner and still adapt to this togetherness style of living, but you must, to some extent, be a *conformist* loner. Each condominium association has its own rulings governing virtually every aspect of life within the community, but outside your own four walls. Read everything, or have your lawyer read, and ask him to check special points that are of concern to you. If you plan to install a lime-green awning over your front door, for example, you will probably not be allowed one. You could be restricted from having a bird bath on your front lawn. And don't even *think* about a satellite dish! None of that may bother *you*, but it annoys some folks, particularly those who have owned their own homes and are not at all used to being told, "Only white curtains, shades, or blinds are allowed at the windows."

Being told how you may decorate is one thing. More seriously, a condominium association's rulings may state no pets. Or no home business where there is traffic from the people you are serving. Rules prohibiting children are now unenforceable, except in complexes designed for senior citizens, but there is still the occasional lawsuit. Do you have a boat, or a recreational vehicle? Note whether you will be prohibited from parking either of them in your driveway. In a condo you can sell to anyone you choose, unlike the cooperative, where new buyers must have approval of the cooperative board.

WHO'S IN CHARGE HERE?

You are, that's who. That can be one of the major adjustments for those who come from apartment life. If you are used to calling the building superintendent when there is a problem in your apartment, you will have to adjust to the fact that while you might be living in what looks like an apartment, there is no super. There is no building manager or managing agent you can call when a faucet drips. It is your responsibility to have it repaired, or not, just as it is your problem in a private home.

All of this is a tricky area, however, which is why your community's bylaws are likely to be such a hefty volume. Let's take a burst pipe as an example. It is the responsibility of the association to repair a malfunction if it is caused by a problem in the main or branch pipes serving your apartment. What occurs within your own four walls—such as a dripping faucet or a problem pipe within your unit—is for you to repair. Now, if you notified the association of a plumbing problem within the common walls, and they did not pay quick attention and your carpeting was ruined by a leak or burst pipe, the association is then likely to be responsible for the damage.

You must also allow access to your apartment in order to get that leak fixed. If you refuse, you could be responsible for the cost of repairs to all of the apartments involved! And if the workers must break through a wall in your unit in order to get to leaking pipes that are staining someone else's walls, you must allow them access. The association is then required to repair your walls and leave the area clean. Whether they must redecorate that wall is questionable. Your homeowners insurance policy should include a clause for redecorating costs in the event of such a necessary breaking of walls between apartments.

Your responsibilities are not exactly those of a tenant or of a totally free owner, either. You are all mutually dependent on one another. So you can't call the super when most things go wrong. On the other hand, you do not have to shovel your way from the front door to the street and beyond with each snowfall, either. Or mow the grass and trim the hedges around your unit. Or paint the exterior.

Beware of Overbuilding!

The most important point you can take away from this chapter is the warning that, while condo buying can be quite successful, it can be almost disastrous in some situations. The huge amount of overbuilding of condo complexes in some parts of the country, and in some parts of any town or city, for that matter, has brought a glut of units to the market. You have to be very careful you do not buy in a saturated area, where it will be difficult to sell when you want to move on. And since this is your first home, you probably will not stay in that community for more than a few years.

Selecting the Right Condo

Most condo complexes do look, well, nice. Is that enough, you wonder? Unfortunately, it is not. Even neat and clean can have a variety of meanings.

Let's say you notice that in some communities maintenance could be better. Nothing outrageous, but the trim around the exterior doors and windows needs a coat of paint. And some of the mortar between the bricks outside is crumbling. Does that mean the association is lax about maintenance? It could be, although it is more likely there are no funds for repairs! The reasons for poor maintenance follow.

READING THE FINANCIAL STATEMENT

Major repairs and improvements in a condo must be paid for by special assessments to the unit owners. It is important that a healthy condo community have a contingency fund for emergency expenses and a reserve for future improvements or repairs. A portion of each unit owner's maintenance fee should be put into these funds.

Read through the financial statement to see if there have been any recent special assessments. Ask members of the board and the management company if any major changes or repairs are being contemplated. How much are they likely to cost? What sum is being held in reserve for them? How much more will be raised through special assessments?

In the same area as not spending money because they do not have it, some communities do not spend because they hate to part with it. Sometimes there is a disagreement over how money is to be spent and time passes and it just is not allocated at all. In the meantime, the complex starts to look just a little shabby and then a little bit more.

You may want to pay an accountant to explain to you these and all other financial details for the community that interests you. This is a very, very important consideration. You want to be sure the community spends money wisely, both for your enjoyment of life there now, and for resale value when you decide to sell.

ABOUT TENANTS

Condominium units are frequently bought for investment purposes. In most condo communities there are a number of tenants living in apartments there. Indeed, some have a very high percentage of renters. *Owners* make the best occupants, however, because it's their money, their pride, and hope for future appreciation of the unit that is on the line.

Many mortgage lenders will not make loans on condos where more than 50 percent of the units are leased to renters. Before you buy a condo, ask a member of the board or a representative of the management company about the ratio of owner-residents to tenants. Too many owner-investors could sway important decisions at a unit owners' meeting, and, because they are not living there, vote against major improvements to the community. It can also be more difficult to band together everyone living in the complex for community projects, social programs, and the like. Tenants often do not care what is going on around them.

GETTING EVEN NOSIER

Once you have narrowed your condo choice down to two or three communities, visit them often. Drive around at night to check lighting, and again in the morning to have a look at rush-hour traffic.

Walk around the grounds and talk to at least three residents. They will usually be happy to chat about the good points of their community, and about any problems and looming expenses. Is there a community newsletter lying around in the laundry room, or on a clubhouse table? Help yourself. Read about the residents to get some idea whether this is a place where you will feel at home.

Condo owners' principal complaints about their homes seem to be in the area of poor soundproofing between units. Be aware of this potential problem in going through apartments. If there is no one upstairs or next door during your visits, come back in the evening, when there are television sets and stereos going. If need be, go next door and ask that resident to turn on his or her television at normal sound. If you can hear noises from adjacent units, you'd be wise to keep on shopping.

Buying Into a New Community

First, be certain that what you are buying into is not in a condo-overbuilt part of town. Another major consideration is maintenance fees. Developers can lowball maintenance charges initially, both to attract buyers and because they do not know accurately at that stage what maintenance actually will be. If the builder is guaranteeing no maintenance for two years, how will you know what these charges will be at the end of that time and if you can afford them?

At what point will the developer turn over the complex to the unit owners? If the developer holds onto too many units for too long, the condo association does not become an independent entity. If he continues to own more than a few condos after the turnover to residents, he can still influence the board of directors, with his voice being far louder than the individual unit owner's.

Another point: recreational facilities are almost always the last part of a complex to be constructed. Sometimes the developer never gets around to them. Are you sure this builder *will* put in that pool? Will you have to pay a special fee for its use? This happens sometimes to buyers who think their monthly maintenance fee covers the use of the pool and tennis courts, and even holding parties in the clubhouse. Then they are hit with a $500 annual fee to join a "club" so that they can use these amenities.

For More Information

If you are seriously about to shop for a condominium, you can contact your state Department of Business Regulations, or your state Board of Realtors for a "how to buy a condo" pamphlet, which most professional groups offer at no charge.

The Cooperative Lifestyle

Not as common as condominiums, cooperatives are run totally differently. A cooperative apartment, to take one point, is considered personal property and not real estate.

All of the unit owners in a cooperative building purchase shares in the corporation that owns and runs the co-op. When you buy your unit, you automatically become a co-owner and have a proprietary lease on that unit.

There is a monthly maintenance fee, which includes the same general charges that a condo owner pays, but co-op owners also pay their proportionate share of the building's mortgage, if there is one. Those parts of the monthly maintenance charge are tax deductible.

To buy a co-op apartment, you must be approved by the board of directors. So, when you sell, of course, you must find a buyer who will be given the green light by the board.

Because co-ops are considered personal, not real property, there is no mortgage if you want to buy. You obtain a secured co-op loan, the security being the certificates of your stock in the corporation. You can shop around for the best loan rates, which would, of course, include both fixed- and adjustable-rate packages. The interest on co-op loans is tax deductible.

THE NONPROFIT CO-OP

Occasionally you will come across a cooperative run on a not-for-profit basis, with government or private association backing. In these apartments, if you are approved for residency according to their income ceilings, you make a nominal downpayment—perhaps several hundred dollars—and your monthly maintenance is a reasonably low figure. When you are ready to sell, the downpayment is returned to you, along with some fair market interest, and that will be that.

The nonprofit co-op can be a step toward having your own home in that it does offer a sense of ownership, and it could allow you to save toward a downpayment on the next place, putting toward that sum your co-op downpayment and its interest. But by definition, nonprofit co-ops are certainly not going to return you very much money, no matter how long you stay and no matter how popular these apartments are where you live.

Which Is Better, Condo or Co-Op?

Both can be wise choices for a starter home, if they are chosen after careful thinking and preparation. The condo, however, because it is real estate and is owned free and clear without the strings of a corporation, comes out ahead. However, the region of the country has something to do with this equation. In New York City, for example, there are far more cooperatives than condominiums. However, in appreciation and ease of selling, depending on that all-important factor, location, both would have to defer to the single-family house.

Tips to Remember

- Beware of areas overbuilt with condominium complexes.
- Check for soundproofing—the major complaint of condo owners.
- Be sure to talk with as many residents as you can in the complex that interests you.
- Go over carefully—or have your lawyer look closely at—all documents presented to you, especially those that spell out the community's financial situation.
- In a brand-new condo complex, where only a few units are yet open, be even more careful about buying. Look principally at the reputation of the developer.
- Also in brand-new communities, remember that you can negotiate with the developer over price, over help with closing costs, with upgrades to your unit, over *anything* connected with the sale.

FOURTEEN
Auctions and Distressed Properties

Auctions and distressed properties are no longer real estate esoterica. They now present a reasonable homebuying opportunity for the average househunter. One program stands out among the others these days: the Resolution Trust Corporation (RTC).

How the RTC Can Help You Buy

The Resolution Trust Corporation is the name of the government-backed entity that is selling properties acquired from failed thrift associations. The failed savings and loan institutions around the country left portfolios of bad loans that resulted in massive property holdings for the RTC. This federal agency was created to dispose of the land and buildings the government found it owned when it foreclosed on some of its loans. The amount of real estate is staggering. Although the RTC has been aggressively selling properties for more than two years now, it still has holdings valued at nearly $20 billion. While most of its real estate is in the southwest, there are properties all over the country.

Virtually every home held by the RTC is sold at auction. And are there bargains! Some homes have sold for $1,000! Admittedly, these are not in prime residential neighborhoods. And it should be pointed out, too, that other houses sell at full market value. The better homes, naturally, have more bidders, which translates into higher prices. Still, there are many solid houses in attractive neighborhoods sold for what anyone would consider an excellent price. If the house is not a steal, the financing is certainly a bargain: low downpayment, no points, no closing costs.

You have probably seen articles in your local paper the day after an RTC auction. Young couples are hugging each other, with the headline reading something like "Some Find Dream Homes at RTC auction." Perhaps you have seen a segment on your local TV news about an RTC auction held that day in your area. The on-scene reporter no doubt interviews someone, or several persons, who were successful bidders for RTC homes.

Here is a thumbnail picture of what is available from the RTC, and how you can make inquiries into their marketing program. You might decide to attend the next auction in your area and perhaps pick up a little something.

Properties. Virtually everything that comes under the heading of real estate can be sold by the RTC: houses, condominiums, income-producing properties, hotels, stores, vacant land, and so on.

Registration. You must be preregistered in order to bid on any property, and in many cases in order to be in the same room where bidding takes place.

Qualifications. About half of the properties sold at any one auction are termed "conventional." This means that there are no income restrictions for bidders. The other half, called "affordable," do carry qualifications. These are homes priced at $67,500 and below, and to qualify to bid on them, shoppers must have an income no higher than 115 percent of the median income for their area. This can be quite high, however. In New Jersey, to take one example, you need to earn as much as $38,500 per household.

If you want to bid, you will be required to furnish, before the day of the auction, tax returns that are requested, a recent pay stub, and documentation revealing how much debt you have and your ability to repay it. Eligibility also depends on the size of the house sought.

Previewing. You can walk through the properties coming up for bid; you would not want to bid on anything you have not seen! Many houses, you will find, are vacant. Many need work, sometimes a lot of work. You will have to calculate renovation costs into how high you are willing to bid for the property itself. By all means take a house inspector along with you if you feel you need a professional opinion about repairs. In a few parts of the country, the RTC has been experimenting with offering warranties for some buyers, with plans to expand this coverage eventually. It might be available in your area.

Up-Front Money. On the day of the auction, you will need $1,000 (conventional) or $500 (affordable) to secure a bidder's card. You will hold up that card to the auctioneer when you want to make a bid. If your bid is successful, you pay—right then—the balance of either 3 percent for affordable homes or 10 percent for conventional.

Mortgages. For affordable housing, the federal government will provide a loan at market interest over 30 years, after a second credit check is concluded. Those buying conventional properties must supply financing, which can come from any lender they select.

Bidder Default. If the highest bidder defaults for any reason, the second-highest bidder will be contacted, or the property will be put back on the block for the next auction.

Real Estate Agents. If you are working with one, she can help you with RTC properties (her commission will be paid by that agency). You do not need an agent, however, to buy an RTC house.

For more information call the RTC's toll-free information line: 1-800-782-3006.

Distressed Properties

These are houses and condominiums where the owners have defaulted in paying their mortgage, property taxes, or water bills.

In the area of nonpayment of property taxes and water bills, you can contact your local tax collector, or other public official who conducts the tax sales, and ask about the next auction of these properties. After you see the list and investigate the addresses, you might contact your lawyer to see if you can purchase the property directly from its owner who is about to lose it.

There are few points you should know, however. For one, owners themselves sometimes manage to come up with delinquent payments, and save their homes before auction time but after their properties are publicly listed; so, some of the addresses you see on the tax collector's list will never actually go to auction. Also, most houses have mortgages, and mortgage lenders do not allow their properties to go on the block for unpaid taxes. The lender will pay the taxes, and then foreclose the property. Finally, this is a complicated arena for the neophyte. After your lawyer explains city tax sales, you might want to forgo this option.

The U.S. Department of Housing and Urban Development (HUD) also sells its foreclosures (houses taken for nonpayment of FHA-backed loans). The houses are sold through sealed bids, with financing arranged through a conventional mortgage lender and insured by the FHA. Downpayment requirements are as low as $100 with some incentive programs. Buyers can finance up to 100 percent of the closing costs, including the initial mortgage insurance premium required by the FHA. Buyers can ask HUD to pay some of the closing costs, and the agency will help with some repair costs. Many of these homes need *work*. As one agency spokesperson put it, "When you buy a house well below market price, you have to expect to put in some sweat equity." Call the number listed on the advertisement you see for more information, or call toll-free the HUD Homes Information System at 1-800-366-4582 any time.

Still more houses: You might contact the Department of Veterans Affairs for their list of VA foreclosures. The Federal National Mortgage Corporation (Fannie Mae) has homes for sale it acquired through foreclosure. You can call Fannie Mae at 1-800-553-4636 weekdays during business hours. Or you can write to Fannie Mae Foreclosed Properties, P.O. Box 13165, Baltimore, MD 21203.

In the private sector, houses are also sold by banks who have taken them back for mortgage delinquencies and other nonpayments (such as those mentioned earlier). You can contact the real-estate-owned, or REO, department of any bank and ask them for a list of their foreclosed properties. Some banks deal directly with prospective buyers for these houses, whereas others assign a real estate broker to handle the sales.

The possibilities here will probably slack off as lenders begin to see the results of their more stringent financing regulations take effect for the end of the decade. Right now, however, you stand to profit.

If you are on a very tight budget, you would be remiss in not following through on at least some of these suggestions. By reading the rest of this book you will learn how to judge a neighborhood, how to tell a good house from a poor one, how to tell if a house needs too many "bad" repairs versus "good" ones, and so forth. You will be an educated consumer who can separate the wheat from the chaff, and there is wheat out there in this particular arena!

Some distressed properties follow the usual route of home sales—through a real estate agency. Sealed offers are the choice of other sellers. Many houses are sold through auctions.

Auction Fever

Auctions are now almost commonplace. However, before attending one with the serious objective of buying a house, you will have to do some homework. Acquire all of the printed material on the sale, for instance (known as the bidder's kit), and visit the homes that interest you. Auctions are conducted as each auction company sees fit. Some are very splashy indeed (I attended an RTC auction that featured local high school girls dressed as auction company cheerleaders, complete with pom-poms, going through several rounds of spirited cheers at each intermission). Still, with all of the variables, there are still some constants. Here is what to remember.

• There are two golden rules at auctions. One is *caveat emptor*, or buyer beware. The second is As is—where it is. And it means just that: there are no refunds, exchanges, or adjustments at auctions. Keep this in mind as you raise your hand or card to bid.
• Be careful that you do not get so carried away by the

adrenelin-pumping proceedings that you overbid. Set a firm limit before the auction of your top offer for any property. You can arrive at that figure by comparison shopping at similar houses for sale in the nonauction arena.

• Once proceedings start, they move quickly. There might be a few minutes of rest between house number 72 and house number 73, but once the bidding starts on 73, it can be over in less than a minute. If you want number 73, you have to move rapidly. There is no time to agonize over whether to increase your bid. The auctioneer's chant is also likely to be unfamiliar and distracting to the novice auction attendee.

Pay *very* close attention. It will help if the property you want is not one of the opening two or three, so that you can become familiar with the speed of the process before *your* home comes on the block.

• Be very sure you are bidding on the property you want. With the speed of the proceedings, mixups do occur.

• Be certain the house you want will be delivered vacant. Government-sold properties usually are, but other sales might not be.

• Be *very* concerned about the title. Will you own the house free and clear?

• Don't be shy. You will have to speak up for the house you want. If you are afraid you will not be able to speak up loudly, or perhaps are concerned that your reflexes are too slow, bring a friend who can do the bidding for you.

• Be sure you know what type of auction you are attending. In an absolute auction, the seller requires no minimum bid, and the highest bidder automatically wins the right to purchase the property. These are the most desirable for buyers and tend to attract the largest crowd. Another type is the minimum bid auction, where sellers agree to sell at the highest bid above an established minimum price. Minimum bid auctions can be good for buyers if the stated minimums are low enough. Bidding usually quickly surpasses the minimum, but once the minimum has been reached the auction is "absolute" because the property is then sold to the highest bidder. Sealed-bid auctions require buyers to submit sealed bids by a set deadline. Afterward, they are opened and the highest-price bid is awarded the house. In a reserve auction, the seller reserves the right to accept or reject the highest bid. This one is not too appealing to buyers, obviously.

• There are many attendants in the auction room to help bidders. Ask them any questions you have.

• Ask in advance how the auction that interests you handles the actual buying of the homes. Some are strictly cash sales. You will almost certainly be required to pay some small amount of money in order to bid. Be sure you understand whether, if you are a winning bidder, you will be given an allotted time after the sale to secure financing, or whether you must be prequalified before the auction.

• With some auctions an on-site lender can offer good financing terms because this institution expects to finance dozens, or hundreds, of homes sold during the sale. Ask about financing, of course, but shop around to see if you can better this type of mortgage package.

• Depending on where you live, you might have the right to cancel your purchase within an allotted number of days following the sale.

Tips to Remember

- Do not bid on property you have not visited in person.
- Remember that you are buying "as is."
- Compare values before bidding, so that you get a sense of the worth of the properties that interest you.
- Try for the best financing you can secure, the way you would with any home purchase.
- Keep rehabilitation costs in mind.
- Be prepared to close quickly. Speed is the reason for auctions.

FIFTEEN
Finding the Land
If You Want to Build

Wait, it's not possible to build my own house when I'm not sure I can afford a home at all, is it?

Absolutely. For some of you, building *some* styles of homes can be quite cost cutting, as you will see in the next few pages. First, of course, comes finding the lot on which to build a house.

The Easier Way
to Acquire a Lot

Some of you may already own a small plot of land. This immediately lowers your total homebuilding cost. Or perhaps you have had half an acre in the family that no one is using. This sounds funny, but it is surprising how many folks buy a parcel of land with no clear intention for its use. They just like the idea of owning land. If you have such a relative, you might be able to purchase his or her parcel inexpensively. Perhaps Uncle Harry is darned sick of paying taxes on his quarter acre and can't seem to sell it on the open market. In you step, his white knight, willing to take it off his hands—for a price.

Or perhaps your folks will join you in shopping for a lot that can be subdivided. You can build on yours; they can hold theirs or sell it to another would-be homebuilder.

Another thought. Does anyone in your family own a lot

that could be split into two parcels, so that you could build on one? You will, however, have to be very sure this is legitimate zoning-wise. *Can* the land be legally subdivided? Will you all have to apply for a zoning variance? This is an instance in which you could, if the location isn't at the high end of the scale, purchase the lot at a reasonable cost from a family member.

When You Have No Land

Frankly, this chapter is not likely to work for you if you have to spend a lot of money for land before building. But if you live in a part of the country where land prices are still relatively inexpensive, or at least parcels that are off the beaten track, then buying a lot and erecting a manufactured home on it can quite cleverly ease you into homeownership at minimal cost.

If you go land shopping, keep in mind that costs for vacant acreage have been rising steadily. Do not be so eager to buy and build that you make a serious error with the lot you select.

First, you should know that not all land is valuable. Yes, you can pay $4,000 for a one-acre lot probably somewhere near you, but it might be impossible to build a home on that lot. Since you are on a budget, you probably cannot afford to buy in an established neighborhood, or even in farm country, where land is being sold to developers in parcels of thousands of acres apiece, if it is being sold at all.

A Buyer's Checklist

You're not discouraged? Good. Here are some important points to note when you go shopping for a home site.

• First, you might check the properties the Resolution Trust Corporation is selling at auctions in your area. They do sell vacant land, and you might be able to pick up a small parcel at a very good price. There is more about RTC auctions and how they work in Chapter 14.

• Look at environmental concerns. It will pay to check into what your state environmental agency is planning to buy for "land bank" or other purposes, and where it will be putting a moratorium on development. Buy too close to a major highway and you might find that the Highway Department is planning to widen a road . . . right into your parlor. Check as many Master Plans and environmental agency reports as you can for the area you are considering.

• Can this land be used as a homesite? What type of permit must be obtained? Are there water and sewer hookups? Is your lot large enough, according to local zoning laws, for construction of a home?

This point is *very* important. I have known of several people who have been dismayed (frantic might be more accurate) to learn that the lot they have purchased is too small, according to local government restrictions, for the house they want to build—or for *any* house. Surely you would prefer to avoid this aggravation by just making sure that the lot you buy is large enough for any house, particularly the one you have in mind. In this area, check also whether the lot is too steep for building.

• There is soil to consider. You might have to add topsoil, or take some away from your lot. If there is rock too close to the soil, this will add to the expense of the foundation, or make it totally impractical. A high water table, or a ground not stable enough to support a house, could run into still more expense. Be especially wary of acreage over a landfill, where flooding can occur frequently as that water table rises.

• Can you erect a manufactured home—your likely, most affordable choice—on the lot? There are some municipalities with regulations against them.

• Utilities are another point to check. Is the lot you are considering serviced by public sewer and water? If not, you will need a septic system and a well.

• Be sure that you get clear title to the land.

• Will you be landlocked? The selling of landlocked lots is illegal in many states. Small plots in the middle of nowhere that can be reached only by helicopter cannot be marketed anymore. There must be an access road.

• What will be going up around you? Check local plans to see what development is on the books, and ask around to see what's in the talking stages for the acreage around the lot you have selected.

• What about the shape of the lot? The more road frontage on an already completed thoroughfare, the more valuable the piece of land will be. The more expense required to develop the land, the cheaper your purchase price should be.

• Do not forget resale value. Being plunked in the woods far from even the nearest hamlet might suit you fine. But when it comes time to sell, will you find a buyer with a similar preference?

• Financing is important, of course. Many sales of land are cash only. The most common means of financing is with the seller holding a short-term mortgage. Balloon loans are a possibility. You might be able to buy land on time through an installment land-purchase contract, where you agree to pay the seller the purchase price in installments over a period time. Title does not pass to you until you have made all payments, or at least a considerable number of them. Naturally, you will not build on land you do not yet own.

• Finally, we cannot forget the local political entity where you buy. If you are buying far out into the country, learn to whom you report building plans, requests, problems, and so on. Be sure you know jurisdictions, town borders, county lines, and the like. If you have to appear before a zoning board or a city council meeting to petition for a zoning variance, try to get a reading on these people. How do they feel about development, even on the small scale you are planning? Are you likely to win your variance?

Once you have a practical, buildable, affordable lot, you need an affordable house to plunk on that land. You are likely to choose a manufactured home, and can read all about them in the next chapter.

Tips to Remember

- Not all land is valuable.
- Be sure that you can build a house on the lot that interests you.
- Be sure that you can build the house you *want* on that lot.
- Check local planning and environmental agencies to see what, if anything, is going to be built around you.
- Picture the house you are building, and the lot that interests you, and consider the resale value of the entire package in its locale.

SIXTEEN
The Very Affordable Manufactured Home

There are many affordable variations on this style of housing. They are handsome single-family (or condominium) communities, brand-new and nicely landscaped. Some of those complexes are the traditional site-built styles, but others have been "built" entirely in a factory. They are produced in sections that can include even carpeting, and then shipped to the building site, where the parts are assembled to form a house.

Some manufactured houses are very plush and are virtually indistinguishable from site-built homes. Others are quite large, but simpler in style. Still other models are small, carry low price tags and resemble new, 1990s versions of the single-width mobile homes of the 1970s and even earlier.

Manufactured homes used to be called mobile homes, but now, in that they are permanent residences, this term is no longer used. That fact was recognized by the U.S. Congress in 1980 when it changed the name to manufactured homes in all of its federal laws and publications. You might see *mobile* around in some older parks, however, and used by some retailers who feel buyers still relate to the word.

Homebuyers choose manufactured homes for one simple reason: They are usually less costly than site-built homes of similar size. An average three-bedroom, two-bath multisection manufactured home loaded with amenities will cost about $40,000, including setup or installation. Larger homes can carry $100,000-plus price tags. Manufacturers usually offer a variety of architectural styles. Carports and garages are extra. Land is not included in those costs, of course.

You can build on your lot if the area you have in mind will permit manufactured homes according to local housing codes, or you can purchase an already built manufactured home in a new-home community. You can also buy a house from a dealer and have it put in a planned manufactured-home community.

Another option is buying a manufactured home and placing it in a *rental* community, where you lease the land beneath the house. You would have to look into this choice very carefully. Will you have a written lease for the land? For how long? How will the financing of your home work? How much are the utility hookup charges? What about the community's rules and regulations? Can you live with them? Who handles maintenance there? Are there special requirements when you want to sell? What if the owner of the community wants to sell his land? Will you then have to move your home? Will you be able to move it where you choose, or will local zoning laws deter you?

Who's Who Here

There are fine distinctions between the several types of factory-built homes. You will need to know *what* you want to buy when you talk to those in the industry. Here is how these folks define their products.

Manufactured Homes. Arrive at your building site on a chassis (wheels, axles, and hitches). They must adhere to standards complying with a federal code set by the U.S. Department of Housing and Urban Development (HUD).

Modular Houses. Are built on a frame that is tucked to your site, and that frame serves as the foundation. Some modulars, however, are built on a chassis. Modular homes must follow standards set by state governments.

Prefabricated. Refers to wall systems and other parts of a home that are built in a factory and assembled on-site. Actually, some parts of a site-built home can be made in a factory and then put together with the rest of the house.

Precut. Certain parts of a house are cut in a factory in volume, and variances in sizing are factory controlled. For example, in site-built homes wall studs can be of sizes that could vary by one-eighth inch or even less, whereas precut, factory-made parts will all be exactly the same.

Kit Homes. Come in pieces, sort of like Lincoln Logs, right down to the nails you need. You can purchase domed home and log cabin styles, but give serious thought before going for either of these selections. The domed home might be a neighborhood oddity, and take you years to sell when you want to move. Log cabins can be excellent choices—if they are plunked in the right location. This means country, of course, rather than city. Almost always even suburban streets are inappropriate. Erect the house where it stands out negatively and you can anticipate a problem come resale time.

Mobile Homes. A term not used officially anymore. A HUD code enacted in 1976 deemed any of these styles built after that year manufactured homes. Pre-1976 homes continue to be termed mobile. For purposes of simplification in

these pages, the term *manufactured* will be used throughout, with mobiles discussed separately later.

Where to Buy
a Manufactured Home

If you want to purchase a home that is already built, or,
more correctly, assembled, you will shop at existing or
brand-new planned communities, just as you would for a
site-built house. Ask at the sales office of the developments that interest you which of the two construction
styles that community features.

If you own land and want to have a manufactured home
put on your lot, you can contact one of the more than 100
companies nationwide that build these houses. They are
represented by thousands of retailers around the country.
The company you call can put you in touch with the
retailer nearest you. Some manufacturers have their own
sales centers in certain parts of the country, too, where
you can also buy. For the names of manufactures, you can
contact the Manufactured Housing Institute. Their address is given at the end of this chapter.

Financing

If a manufacturing home is permanently set on a foundation, and is sold with land or erected on land owned by
the new homeowner, it usually can be financed with a real
estate mortgage. Mortgages can be secured from the same
variety of lenders as any site-built home, including FHA
and VA sources. The key here is that the home and land
are considered a single real estate entity under state law.

Manufactured homes on *rented* land, and houses that are considered personal property rather than real estate (mobile homes, for one, come under this classification) are treated differently, and are not financed as real estate with a home mortgage. Manufactured home retailers can arrange financing for these purchases, or you can shop around for better terms at banks and other lending institutions in your area. The interest rate on a manufactured home loan is usually a few percentage points higher than on a real estate mortgage. The FHA, the FmHA, and the Department of Veterans Affairs (VA) also have programs for manufactured homes.

Mobile Homes

True mobile homes, erected before 1976 and usually situated in mobile home communities, are another housing option. Some of these "parks" are very attractive and the homes in them can appreciate slightly in value rather than depreciate, the way the old single-width mobiles have in the past. Not at the same pace as traditionally built houses, though. We are not talking "trailer camps" here, but parks of usually double- and even triple-width units; homes that are almost never moved from their original site. If you are interested in mobiles, you do want to see some return on your investment so that you can use that money toward your next purchase. Shop carefully, and take heed of the suggestions made earlier for buying on rented land. Remember, too, that pre-1976 homes were not subject to the same strictures as HUD-regulated, post-1976 manufactured homes.

Resale

One of the cardinal points made throughout this book, as you have noted, has been keeping an eye on resale value when you buy *any* home. The same is true here. Location means virtually everything when you put up the For Sale sign, but a quality home kept in good condition runs a close second. Whether you can afford a top-of-the-line manufactured home or a very simple style, make sure that there is a resale market for it in the area you choose.

For More Information

Manufactured Housing Institute
1745 Jefferson Davis Highway, Suite 511
Arlington, VA 22202
Telephone: (703) 979–6620

MFI has reams of printed material for the consumer on manufactured and modular homes. They can also put you in touch with your state MFI office. (You might be able to find the latter in the white pages of your phone book. The office is usually in the state capital.)

Building Systems Council
National Association of Home Builders
15th and M Streets NW
Washington, DC 20005

The Council can offer information about domed and log cabin homes.

How to Buy a Manufactured Home, is available for 50 cents from the Consumer Information Center, Dept. 429W, Pueblo, CO 81009.

Tips to Remember

- Buy from a quality manufacturer. Your home is only as good as that company's product and reputation.
- Keep an eye on resale potential. You will want to come away from this purchase with at least some market appreciation, to help toward the downpayment on your next home.
- If you want to erect a manufactured home on land you own, be sure that local ordinances will allow you to do so.

PART V
HOW TO BUY THE HOME YOU'VE CHOSEN

SEVENTEEN

The House Inspection: When? By Whom? How Much?

This chapter is directed at everyone buying a resale home, whether that structure is 150 years old or just three. It is for condominium and cooperative buyers as well.

One of the contingencies of a sale, written in your contract to buy, can be a house inspection by anyone you designate. This has become such a common practice in the last half dozen years or so that it is almost assumed by the seller and real estate agent that you will want a professional inspection. And you will, you will.

One of the brightest ideas to come along in the last decade has been having professionals look at a house before the buyer plunks down—or mortgages for most of his life—the enormous amount of money it takes to buy a home.

House inspections can cost anywhere from $150 to $500, with the average of $250. This is a small expense compared to an investment of perhaps $100,000 or more. You do *not* have every house that interests you inspected. Call a professional only after you have made an offer to buy, the offer has been accepted, and you have signed a sales contract. It is rare for buyers to have more than one house inspection during the entire househunting experience.

Sometimes lenders will require a professional inspection before approving a mortgage loan. This is not to be confused with an appraisal, which is always called for by lending institutions. An appraiser, chosen by the lender, does not usually go inside the house, however, and is concerned with the neighborhood, and the overall appearance of the property and whether it represents a safe investment for the lender.

The most important reason for your having an inspector is bringing to light any important problems in that house, disasters already there or those about to happen. You may still buy the house, but you have room to negotiate the price if you can say to the owner, "Well, the house inspector says the roof's in very bad shape. He estimates it to be ten or eleven years old, so it's about due for replacement." Your comments can open negotiating for a lower price and/or repairs. Also, it is important that you never be so in love with a house that you cannot see its flaws. Therein lies potential financial disaster.

No house is perfect, however. It is pointless to search for a home in mint condition, thinking that this is how you can save money in repairs. Mint condition homes are extremely rare. On the other hand, just because a house needs work is no reason not to buy it—as long as you are aware of its defects and what they are likely to cost you, either immediately or a few years down the road.

The second good reason for a house inspector, especially for the first-time buyer is that he (most are men) will help you become acquainted with this huge place that is about to become yours.

More and more sellers are offering prospective buyers home inspection reports that *they* have ordered and paid for (especially in a very slow market). If you are interested in a home that has such a report, good for you. You will save the expense of getting your own inspector, and you can take that report around the house with you, checking points made by the inspector.

When You Inspect a House

As mentioned earlier in this chapter, there are two inspections, one by you and one by a pro. You will go through many homes in your search for the one to buy. Some you will be in and out of in 5 minutes, maybe less. Some you will walk through, pause here and there, perhaps ask some questions of the agent, and take the agency's computer printout on the place so you can remember the details about pricing, property taxes and the like.

On your second or even third visit to a house that seriously interests you, you will want to get down to the nitty gritty. You call your real estate agent and say you would like to see 333 Appletree Lane again. On this visit you will wear old clothes, and bring some important equipment with you: a flashlight with a bright beam, a yardstick or tape measure, marble or small ball, a pocket-knife or ice pick, and a pad and pencil.

Before you head for Appletree Lane you might want to jot down some questions you still need answered by the sellers. Perhaps they will be away, but the real estate agent can relay these queries for you. You might also want to note any special problems or concerns you are likely to have with any house you buy. Do you need room for a piano? Will your rather sizable sofa fit against the only solid wall in the living room? Will the girls' room be large enough for twin beds, or will you have to furnish it with bunk beds? This type of thing.

Don't worry, whatever you are checking will be gone over more thoroughly by the house inspector. What you are looking for here are any serious problems that will keep you from wasting time making a bid on the house, having an inspector over, and *then* learning about obvious catastrophes.

Once at the house, here is what you will be looking for:

The Foundation. That is any construction that is below or partly below the ground level and upon which the house is built. It could be a concrete slab, walls and a crawl space, or a full basement. The most common materials in today's construction are concrete, concrete block, and cinderblock. In very old houses, stone is most common. To prevent termite infestation and dry rot, all wood parts of the house should be at least six inches off the ground. Hairline cracks in the slab that are visible as you walk around outside are not usually a cause for alarm. Major separations or extensive crumbling are.

The Crawl Space. A foundation that lifts the house eighteen to thirty-six inches off the ground is called a crawl space. It is most often built of concrete block or cinderblock. The floor of this area is often the ground itself, a situation that can cause serious moisture problems, especially if ventilation is inadequate. At least one foundation wall-ventilator should be built in at each corner with all four being kept open year-round.

A wet crawl space can cause joists (subfloor beams) to rot and can send harmful ground vapors up into the house, causing mildew and dampness. A wet or damp crawl space can often be corrected with adequate ventilation. If the space is floored and heated, venting is unnecessary.

Crawl spaces are difficult to inspect and many homebuyers just do not bother. If *you* don't want to, make sure that your inspector does (some of them want to skip this, too). He should be looking for standing water on the ground, especially near the walls and in the corners. When he pokes at beams, an ice pick should *not* sink into the wood. This is a potential sign of termites or dry rot. He

YOU *CAN* BUY A HOME • 159

should also look about for rodents' nests. They love the darkness of crawl spaces.

The Basement. Here is where you will see more of the working systems of the house than anywhere else. One thing you will be looking for here is dryness. Basement dampness (as opposed to standing water) is often due to condensation. This can be corrected by a dehumidifier.

Seepage from outside ground water is a much more serious problem and can undermine the structural sound-ness of a house. First check for water in the corners. If you see some, it may be due to the faulty positioning of a downspout. Your water problem could be solved by moving, extending, or repairing the downspout. How-ever, such puddles could be the result of a collection of ground water around the footings, a very serious problem that can cause uneven settling. If you see water, suspi-cious stains, or a newly repainted floor and cracks in the foundation walls, you might want to forget about 333 Appletree Lane. Or, if you really want the house, get in the professional inspector quickly.

Beware also of stains on the basement walls. If you see yellowish brown markings at the same level all around the basement, it is probably dried moisture and is likely to be the high-water mark. The basement does flood or has flooded! Overall, be wary of newly painted walls. Sure, many sellers do paint long-overlooked areas when they are getting ready to put out the "For Sale" sign, but it pays to be particularly cautious when you see fresh paint in basement spaces.

If there is a sump pump, ask the owners how it works. Ask where the pump drains. A dry well at some distance from the house is good. Even better, if allowed by your town, is a storm sewer system, in that the water is permanently taken away from the foundation. A pump that takes the water up and out through the basement window does not accomplish much. This is a little like bailing a leaking boat, in that the water is still on the other side of the wall.

If there has been a lot to read here about basements, it is because water in the basement is one of a homeowner's principal fears. It should be one of yours at this stage of the buying process.

All houses settle somewhat, and a few hairline cracks in the foundation are acceptable. But if a footing sinks, leaving the support of the structure uneven, the soundness of the house and every working system in it can be endangered.

Look for large cracks in the foundation walls that can be seen from both inside and outside the basement. A house with a serious settling problem will have doors and windows that bind, and diagonal cracks in the wallboard or plaster, especially above doors and windows. Repairing the problem is very expensive.

Termites. Look for traces of these critters while you are in the basement—and evidence of wood decay and dry rot. Take your ice pick where they are in direct contact with the foundation walls. These contact points between wood and concrete are the most vulnerable to all wood deterioration problems. Problems exist if your blade slips into the wood or if you encounter a spongy rather than a solid resistance.

Termites are not the only little devils gnawing away at a house. Others are such things as powder post beetles. They eat wood the same way termites do. Beware of floors that feel spongy when you walk on them.

A careful eye can save you hundreds, even thousands of dollars. At this stage the price of the house can be lowered, the seller can take on repairs, or you can split the cost. Overlook a trouble spot, buy the house, and there is no question who will write the check for the fixups.

The Working Systems. These are areas where the professional is likely to know more than you. Still, there are some areas even a novice can check.

ELECTRICAL. You can find out whether or not the wiring is adequate by looking around the house. If there is a dishwasher, clothes washer and dryer, a few television sets, electrical stove and oven, central air conditioning, and a computer in the bedroom, you can be reasonably certain the wiring is adequate. Be sure that there are enough outlets. Too many appliances and gadgets plugged into extension cords is a bad sign. Try the light switches. Check to be sure the doorbell rings. If it is broken, this is one repair you can have the seller make before closing. You will need that chime immediately during the busy days of moving in.

Having an electrical system upgraded is certainly possible. It is a somewhat major repair and hard to estimate cost-wise, but it is not something that should put you off buying a house.

HEATING. Is the system safe? Does it provide enough heat? How much does it cost to run? Determining safety is another job for the experts. Seeing if the heating is adequate is something you can both do. You can ask to have the heat turned on, no matter when you are looking at the house. A good way to check the system's efficiency and the weather tightness of a house—and how much staying warm is going to cost you—is to ask the owner of the house for the heating bills for the previous winter and the name of the fuel supplier. Then call the oil or utility company and ask what a typical bill for a house of your square footage would have been for the previous winter. Do the same with central air conditioning if you have never had the system and wonder if this is going to cost you a large sum of money each summer.

PLUMBING. You can examine the condition of exposed pipes, but an inspector will likely know more than you about their condition. Old, iron pipes or lead fittings could need replacement. Also, be sure to run water from faucets and flush toilets. Is the water clear or rusty? Also, look for leaks, low water pressure, and drains that empty too slowly.

There are many other parts of a house you will want to investigate, although the aforementioned are the most important and potentially most costly. For your own purposes you will want to note room sizes, traffic flow patterns, size and state of the kitchen, number of bathrooms and the like. Be sure to look at windows and storm windows, if there are any. If there are none, are you prepared for the high expense of purchasing them? Are the floors level? Test them with the ball or marble you have brought. Do they need refinishing? Any creaky boards? What about the stairs? Any problems there? Are all of the appliances that will stay with the house in working order? Read Chapter 9 for more spot-check tips.

Take almost nothing you see at face value. Paint, as mentioned above, could be hiding problems, and so could new wallpaper in a room or section of a room.

Calling in the Pros

Once you have some idea of the workings of the house that interests you, you can begin negotiating with the seller over price. When you arrive at a figure acceptable to both of you, you can have it written in the sales contract that the sale will proceed subject to a house inspection that proves satisfactory to you.

Now you call in a professional. Perhaps you know a home remodeler in your town, or an engineer who does house inspections. Those folks can be fine, if you are very sure they are qualified to look at *every* area of a house.

Be certain, too, they can be objective and owe no allegiance to a real estate agency or company you might choose to do repair work. In the latter area, for instance, hiring a man or woman who does home repairs would clearly be a conflict of interest and should be avoided. Your best bet: someone who has a contractor's license or experience in residential construction. An engineer might be able to give you advice on repairs and new installations that a house inspection service cannot and is not required to, but you are likely to pay more for the engineer's services.

No matter whom you hire, you should be given a typed report, and quickly. Most companies will have this document in the mail to you in a few days.

How do you find a good inspector? It is best not to ask the seller to recommend one. Don't use the real estate agent's recommendation either, if she supplies only one name. Even the best of people can suggest an inspector who perhaps subconsciously will not make too many waves so that the sale does not fall through and they will not be recommended by that realty agency again.

Some real estate agents supply buyers with a sheet of three or four names and addresses of inspectors/inspection services. They will say those are the companies their customers have been pleased with, or some such comment. This is different, of course, from making just one suggestion, so feel free to check any, or preferably all, of these recommendations.

You can also ask friends and business associates for referrals. In large corporations, personnel offices that handle transfers will often supply the names of inspection firms. You might also call your mortgage lender or your lawyer for recommendations. Finally, in a pinch, you can look to the Yellow Pages. Tell the inspection service you call that you are responding to their advertisement, so that they will know they owe no loyalty to your realty agency or to the seller.

You will find large, nationwide inspection services and small local firms. Neither is necessarily better than the other. You can also look for those who are members of the American Society of Home Inspectors (ASHI), which sets professional standards for its members. Those who are not members—usually small, independent local services—may still be fine.

When you make your initial phone call to an inspector, ask if he actually goes on the roof and gets into the crawl space under the house if it is at all possible. Some do these checks as a matter of course, others will charge extra. Also, testing for radon and asbestos, well-water contamination, or termites will usually cost more than the flat fee. The home inspection service might also direct you to someone else for these reports.

Ask the inspector what type of written report you can expect. If possible, look at a sample. Does it give the ages of specific systems in the house? Does it offer projections of when parts or systems might need repairs? Does it estimate the cost of these repairs and of remedies to existing problems? (Some of these questions you can get answers to by accompanying the inspector on his tour of the house.) Ask whether the inspection company carries any type of liability insurance to cover any damage to your house, or major defects the house inspector does not catch. How long will the inspection take? A general one can run about an hour and a half, a more detailed look of two hours plus is likely to cost more. The house inspector should not comment about the wisdom of your buying a particular house and you should not ask his advice.

It can be wise to call your local Better Business Bureau and your local Department of Consumer Affairs to see if any complaints have been lodged against the service you are thinking of using. Checking with consumer agencies is not a fail-safe way to protect yourself, however. A lack of complaints on file against one company is no guarantee that the outfit does a good job. It just shows that no dissatisfied customers took the time to write letters. You can call the American Society of Home Inspectors at (703) 524-2008 for the names of ASHI members in your area. And the Council of Better Business Bureaus offers the free booklet of tips on home inspection. You can call them at (703) 276-0100 or write them at 4200 Wilson Boulevard, Arlington, VA 22203.

The Condo or Co-Op Inspection

A comprehensive checkup is as important in these housing styles as it is with the single-family home. You can use the same information to look through the unit that interests you. Then call an inspection service to recheck the unit *and* the basement and/or other common areas of the complex. These doors are usually locked. You will probably need permission for entry from the Board of Directors or the building superintendent or managing agent. Do not fail to make the extra effort, however—and remember to go along with the inspector. You may never see these areas again, but what you learn on your tour can help you put your unit into the larger framework of how the entire condo/co-op community works.

Tips to Remember

- A professional house inspection is money well spent. Don't stint here, no matter how tight your budget.
- Avoid engaging anyone who offers to make repairs, or an inspector whose loyalty is apt to be with the seller or your real estate agency.
- No house is perfect. Just know how much imperfection you can live with—or afford to repair.

EIGHTEEN
Negotiating the Price of a Home and Signing a Contract

Realize that while you have done your job properly in securing the right mortgage commitment for you and opening your mind to a wide variety of housing choices, your being able to buy a home when you think you can't afford one will also depend on your negotiating skills. You *will* have to bargain over the price of the home you want, whether you are a stranger to the process or reasonably confident of your skills.

How to Negotiate

First, you are going to determine the fair market value of the house. This is defined as the highest price a ready, willing, and able buyer will pay and the lowest a ready, willing, and able seller will accept. You will do this by comparing the property you want to buy with others in the same area that have been sold in the previous year. When you are ready to start negotiating, ask your realty agent to show you "comparables." In a real estate office this means the listing sheets describing properties that have recently been sold. These sheets contain all of the pertinent information on a property, the original asking price, all of the price reductions, the actual selling price, and the date of the original listing contract (which will tell you how long the property was on the market). Once you have this list, you can check for homes similar to yours. What did they sell for? Were they larger than the one you want? Smaller? Pretty much identical in size and features?

Once you finish that homework, compare what you determine is fair market value for the house with what the sellers are asking. Unless they have underpriced the house (and then you must ask yourself why), their price is likely to be higher than your evaluation price.

Ask yourself why they have set the price that much higher. To allow room for negotiating? Because they have installed new carpeting? They want to be repaid for the newly remodeled $14,000 kitchen? Take the position that the sellers' adding amenities or upgrades does not always add to the resale value of a home.

It is wise to buy a small notebook at this point, and enter all of these figures for the house: asking price, prices of comparables, your ideal price (which would probably be a steal), your fair market estimate, and the absolute top dollar price you would be willing to pay for the house.

Why would you pay a top-dollar price higher than fair market value, you ask? Because fair market value cannot be truly determined until the property is sold. During the negotiating process, it is still an estimate. Even professional real estate appraisers can differ in their fair market value estimates. So leave yourself a margin between your dream price—or steal—and how high you will be willing to go, to allow for negotiating.

Most important of all during this negotiating stage: do not tell your real estate agent your top dollar figure. Remember, the agent represents the seller. Tell her you will be willing to go up to $83,000 for an $85,000 house, and that is probably what you will wind up paying. You have to play your hand close to the vest during the negotiating process.

OTHER CONSIDERATIONS

Besides checking comparables and working the numbers, there are a few other points to keep in mind before you make an offer. One of the more important is gauging the state of the market in your area at the time you want to buy. If it is a hot sellers' market, you will not have as much bargaining power as you would in a slow market. If you are looking in a very trendy and popular neighborhood, there, too, you are not likely to strike a bargain. Be aware of all this so that in the first instance you do not expect an unbelievably good deal, and in the second you do not bid the price up too high.

If the house you want has been on the market a long time, you are more likely to get your price or close to it. (Of course, you will ask yourself why it has been standing so long. Price too high and seller inflexible? Needs much work? Across the street from a filling station?) Also, ask the agent if there have been any price reductions on the house you want to buy. This could indicate a very strong desire to sell and/or a rethinking of the property's value.

YOUR OPENING OFFER, AND SUBSEQUENT OFFERS

Open with your best bid, but be willing to move up another $500 or $1,000 if the house really appeals to you. At the initial stage, ask for as few extras as possible, and be agreeable about the closing date.

How much below asking price should that initial offer be? The often-mentioned figure of 10 percent is really not accurate. There are too many variables, both in the economic picture in your region and the way sellers set prices for their homes. If you want a guideline, make that first offer 10 percent below your fair market value estimate, not the seller's asking price.

You must present a written offer to the seller. An oral

bid is not how things are done here. Your real estate agent will present you with a contract form to sign (short-form binders have become increasingly outdated). This form will contain the date, your name and address and those of the seller's, the price you are offering for the home, a date for closing (which may be changed more than once), signatures of all parties involved, and the amount of the earnest money check you will be required to present as a token of your serious intent. This is usually a minimum of $500, but more often $1,000. Your check should be made out to the real estate agency's trust account, or to the firm that will be handling the closing. Never, never issue a check made out to the sellers.

The form is also likely to include items in the house that will be included with the sale, how the financing is to be handled, and, broadly speaking, what closing fees the buyer and seller will be expected to pay (they will be gone into in more detail later by your lender or your lawyer). There might also be mention of termite inspection, of the promise of clear title, and of adjustments, such as how taxes, water and sewage charges, fuel, utility bills, interest on mortgages (when assumable) and rent (if there are tenants involved) are to be handled between buyer and seller on the date of settlement.

There is usually room on this form, which can run to two pages, for something called "Additional terms, conditions, or addenda." Here is where you will fill in "Subject to review [of the contract] by the buyer's attorney within three (or four) business days of the signing of this contract." This is important. You will want to have your lawyer review the contract in that time, but if you have no lawyer you will still want that clause because it gives you time to back out of the deal if you choose to do so within the allotted time. It does not hurt to buy three or four days' rethinking time.

You will also want to fill in that space the clauses "Buyer securing a mortgage at terms acceptable to buyer," and "Subject to satisfactory house inspection by buyer or buyer's designate within 10 days." If you are moving into a condominium, townhome, patio home, single-family home, or any community where all residents must join a homeowners association, be sure to add "Subject to buyer's inspection of the Horizon Hills Covenants and Restrictions." You don't want to commit yourself to a home and then learn that two dogs are acceptable, when you have three.

If you are buying a home that is presently occupied by renters, or if you are buying a two-family house with a rental unit and you want that unit vacant, insert another clause to the effect that "The house is to be delivered vacant at the closing." In fact, if you expect snags from the existing owners moving out in time for the closing, you might also want that clause inserted in a contract.

In most states a real estate agent must by law present any reasonable offer to the seller she represents; so, if your agent tells you, "Oh, that's far too low," don't listen. The law is on your side. Perhaps the phraseology in your area is "all reasonable offers." Offering $10,000 for a $140,000 house does not constitute a reasonable offer, but offering $90,000 might, depending on the location and condition of the dwelling. Don't be nervous about or ashamed of a low first offer.

HAGGLING

It is unlikely the seller will accept your first offer. Sometimes he or she will come back with a counteroffer, but not usually. They do not want to give away *their* hand either. Are you willing to go higher? If you raise your offer by $500, you might want to ask for some extras now, such as the living room draperies. Still rejected? Offer another $1,000, and request that the closing take place no sooner than eight weeks from the signing of the contract, if that is more convenient for you, or that the seller pay the points you will be charged.

At every stage of bidding, mention to your real estate agent something to the effect that, of course, you like and want the house, but gee, it does need bathroom modernization and you really wanted a two-car, not a one-car garage. You want her to know—and relay to the sellers—that you are not so committed to this house that you will pay *anything* to own it. Your attitude should be, "If this doesn't work out, I'll just go back to looking at more houses. My heart won't be broken."

The back-and-forth negotiating usually goes no more than three rounds before an agreement is reached. This is where a good real estate agent earns her commission! You would not want to be doing this face to face with the seller, and the agent, while collecting her commission from the seller, also realizes without a buyer there will *be* no commission, so she is finely tuned to both the seller's and buyer's feelings during this part of the transaction.

NEGOTIATING WITH FSBOS

When there is no real estate agent involved, when you are dealing with homes that are "for sale by owner," the same principles for negotiating apply, but with a difference. There is, of course, no middle man.

How do you begin? After your second visit to the home you like (the call where you will poke around a bit more than you did on your initial visit), wait a day or two before making an offer, to heighten the seller's anticipation and to make your offer sound well thought out.

To determine fair market value here, go through the

computer printout sheets you have secured from real estate agents for similar properties in the neighborhood. The bargaining process applies here, but sitting down face to face with sellers is always difficult. Keep rational and friendly and remember that your primary tool for acceptance is that fair market value. Your offer hands them a quick sale, no more disruption in having a house on the market, and no sales commission.

Still, they will not likely accept your first price. Back you come with a second bid. This will usually be the fair market value minus the usual real estate commission in the area (probably 6 percent). No, the sellers reply. What would be the point of our deducting the services of an agent when we have no agent?

In the best possible scenario, the buyer and seller will split the real estate commission, and set the selling price between market value and net-to-owner after commission. All of the extras, such as closing dates and financing can be worked out then and there, or with the attorneys for both sides (you will definitely want a lawyer in an FSBO sale). The attorneys will draw up the contract to buy. Do *not* use the same legal counsel as the sellers.

This is how a neat, tidy sale works. But life does not always follow such a script. The sellers may be new to this business, and hold out high hopes for top dollar. When you come up against a stone wall, do not beat your head against it, no matter how much you like the house. Write down your best offer, with your name, address, and phone number, and leave it with the sellers. Tell them to call you if they change their minds, and continue house-hunting. You might want to keep in touch with them from time to time to ask how they are doing. Do not make another offer, but if they do come down a little, perhaps you will be willing to go up a little. This is how negotiating works. Also, never give sellers an earnest money deposit. This check should be handed to your lawyer.

Finding a Lawyer

You are not required to have legal counsel in order to purchase a home, but it is wise for first-time buyers to engage a lawyer. It is very wise to do so if you are buying a condominium or cooperative or any community-type home where you must belong to an owners association. Going through the raft of printed documents—prospectus, rules and regulations, covenants, and so on—should be done by someone trained to look for red lights. That someone should be a real estate lawyer. Do not engage anyone who has another legal specialty. You call in a lawyer at the stage when you have bid on a house and need the lawyer to review the sales contract. Or when you are shopping for a condo, townhome, and the like, and are presented with a raft of printed material about the home that interests you, and need help with explanations of covenants, financial statements, and the like.

How do you find a lawyer? Your real estate agent should be able to help you. Your mortgage lender will probably have some names, too. Or you can call your local bar association and ask for the names of lawyers specializing in real estate, particularly local residential real estate.

When you find a lawyer, ask about fees for reviewing contracts and giving advice. Is this set at an hourly rate? A flat fee? No charge if you go on to use that individual for the house closing? Ask the lawyer what the usual role of counsel is in house closings in your area. Will the lawyer be present at the closing? What is the closing fee?

Remember that lawyers' fees are not set according to any local or state formula. Shop around for the best terms the way you would for any consumer purchase, but also consider the reputation, knowledge, and experience of the lawyer you choose.

Tips to Remember

- Do not let emotion get in the way of prudent, aggressive negotiation. This is especially important when dealing with FSBOs.
- Always keep to yourself the figure that represents the highest offer you will make on a particular house. This has been stressed several times throughout these pages, and is *very* important.
- Before making an offer, note the economic climate of your particular community, comparable sale prices of nearby homes, and how motivated the seller is likely to be (how long the house has been on the market is a good indicator).
- Make your first bid low enough so that if it is snapped up you will not feel you have overpaid.

NINETEEN
All About Homeowners Insurance

Oh no, you say, still more documents to read, legalese to wade through and decisions to make. Now it's insurance.

Well yes, but take heart. What is coming up in these few pages is nowhere near as nervewracking as negotiating for a home, or signing up for a mortgage. This is a decision and process that will make you feel safer against known and unknown perils that could wipe you out financially—and your house literally!—if you tried to go it alone, without a homeowners policy. Do I sound like an insurance sales agent? Ah, but this is one policy everyone can see the wisdom in purchasing.

Lenders will not consider offering you a mortgage if you do not have homeowners insurance from day one. They care about their investment. You will be required to make payments for as long as your home is in their portfolio. In fact, if you let your policy lapse, the insurance company will send a copy of the cancellation to both you and your lender. Your lender might then start foreclosure proceedings if you do not reinstate the coverage, and quickly.

What Is Homeowners Insurance

Shortly after your offer for a home has been accepted and the wheels start rolling toward the closing, your lawyer or real estate agent will tell you to start shopping for homeowners insurance. You will have to show your mortgage holder proof at the closing that you have purchased a homeowners policy and have paid the first premium.

Do shop around for an insurance policy the way you have for a home and a mortgage. Make some phone calls. Your real estate agent may have a suggestion. Indeed, in many agencies there is an insurance branch within the office. By all means speak to that person about coverage, but get two additional written estimates.

You should know that in this field an insurance agent is a representative of a specific insurance company, whereas a broker sells insurance for several companies. Ask at an agency where you carry another form of insurance if they will offer you a lower rate on a homeowners policy because you have other coverage with that carrier. You should also ask whether discounts are offered if you have—or will install—such protective devices as smoke alarms and deadbolt locks. Another money-saving tip: opt for annual premium payments, if you can, instead of monthly or quarterly, which frequently include a service charge.

Varieties of Policies

A basic homeowners policy protects your home, shrubbery, trees, and outside structures from nearly a dozen perils, including fire, theft, vandalism, lightning, and windstorms. A broad policy adds another seven items, including protection against damage from frozen pipes, falling objects, and sprinkler systems—virtually everything but war, nucleur accident, floods, and earthquakes.

Standard homeowners policies in any category also offer peripheral coverage for calamities befalling your home.

For example, if you have to evacuate the house in the event of a fire or some other disaster, the typical policy usually pays your living expenses elsewhere of around 10 percent of your home's coverage.

YOUR CHOICE

You will generally be offered one of three packages, with HO-1 being the most basic and HO-3 the most comprehensive. Note that you are only covered for the misfortunes listed on your policy, which is why it is important to read the document very carefully. Think, too, about the age of the home you are buying, its siting, landscaping, and so on.

The standard homeowner's policy consists of coverage for 100 percent of the replacement value of your home (80 percent is the minimum to consider), plus coverage for your personal belongings and liability coverage to protect you if someone is injured in your home or on your property. The policy should not include land. You can, in all likelihood, build on it again, so do not insure dirt! Similarly, the foundation is likely to be there following almost any calamity. If you do not know what the replacement cost of your home would be, you can ask your insurance agent, or call in an appraiser. It is important that you secure replacement coverage, which is what it would cost to rebuild the home at today's prices.

There are many variations on the homeowners package, and there are limits to certain categories of coverage. Investigate them all. Given the variables of how much the carrier you select charges, how much you are insuring your home for, and the amount of extra protection you want, you can pay anywhere from a few hundred dollars to over $1,000 annually in premiums. The average cost of a policy for a $100,000 house at 80 percent replacement value is $450 a year.

The standard deductible is often $100–200. You can save 10 to 35 percent in premiums if you elect higher deductibles, the highest being about $1,000. Remember, the purpose of this coverage is to protect you from a wipeout of thousands, perhaps hundreds of thousands of dollars. Why saddle yourself with high premiums for years and years if you can well afford to pay out $1,000 if an incident occurs, before the insurance company picks up the rest?

Will your premiums go up if you file a claim? Quite possibly. Also, depending on the amount of your claim(s), and their frequency, a company might decide not to renew your coverage. Or they may ask for the maximum rise in payments allowed by law—and let you find a new insurer.

The Fair Access to Insurance Requirements plan is in effect in more than twenty states, offering insurance to those who have difficulty securing protection for a high-risk property or one situated in a high-risk area. Your real estate agent can tell you more about FAIR.

ON THE PERSONAL SIDE

Your personal possessions are also insured with a standard homeowners policy when you insure the structure itself. This coverage extends to your possessions when you are away from home too, in the event of theft or loss.

The usual coverage for the contents of a home is 50 percent of the home's insured value. So, a house carrying $150,000 worth of insurance will be covered by $75,000 for personal property, which includes furniture and clothing. This is for the standard actual cash value coverage, which deducts for depreciation. You will almost always have to pay extra—perhaps another 10 percent—if you want that property insured at full replacement value.

Then there is liability coverage. Awards for relatively

minor injuries that used to be $100,000 a few years ago, now are $300,000. And this is not the worst that could happen to a guest on your property, as you can imagine. So the $100,000 liability limit, which had been so common for years, has been increased in the last few years. You will probably find that for as little as an additional $20–30 a year in premium costs, you can raise that protection to $300,000 per incident.

You might also give some thought to umbrella coverage. This is liability protection that picks up where both your homeowners and automobile policies leave off. Umbrellas can cost about $150–200 annually for $1 million of coverage, going up to $250 to $300 for as much as $10 million. By all means look into this, even if you do not have a home or lifestyle you think would warrant such protection. Guests slipping on stairs, the cleaning woman on unshoveled snow that has now become ice, the postal carrier seriously bitten by your cute little doggy—all can result in lawsuits. Umbrella coverage includes some libel protection and some coverage if an incident occurs while you are engaged in volunteer work. This is an increasingly litigious society we live in; you might well want to consider an umbrella policy.

SPECIAL ENDORSEMENTS

Do you have a few pieces of heirloom jewelry you want protected? Some silver you value? Most policies will cover up to, say, $1,000 for loss of jewelry, furs, and watches, and up to $2,500 for silverware (figures vary from one carrier to another and according to coverage purchased). But there is often no provision for such special items as antiques, art, and valuable collectibles. They can be covered with the purchase of a personal articles floater, at an additional cost to you. Coverage applies whether or not the articles are in your home at the time of loss. It also includes damage or breakage, which is not covered by the standard homeowners policy. Most standard policies provide coverage for original cash value minus depreciation. You can upgrade your coverage to include replacement cost, a far better protection for you.

What about the home you are buying? Do you feel it is worth more than the amount an insurer is willing to cover? Probably not, if you have struggled to purchase this house. Few starter homes are that lavish. Still, you might be buying a charming, detail-laden, elderly fixer-upper. Possibly certain features, built into the house when it was constructed perhaps more than a century ago, are unique and cannot be duplicated today. The house might even be a designated regional or state landmark. Replacement cost, using modern materials, cannot bring that house back to its original state.

If you have bought a house with some historic or architectural distinction (you probably have not put in thousands of dollars of renovation yet), first have the house appraised professionally before you approach an insurance agent or broker. You will probably have to shop around quite a bit for a policy that takes all of this into account. Insurers are wary of coverage above replacement value because of the fear of arson for profit. Still, finding the right policy is not impossible.

Still More Coverage

There are special insurance packages for even more calamities. Here are four that are most common.

FLOOD INSURANCE

Fire protection comes with a standard homeowners policy, but coverage for floods does not. This usually comes as quite a surprise to a homeowner who suffers flood damage, so you may want to give this type of policy some thought. Your homeowners policy probably *does* protect you against flooding that occurs, say, from a burst pipe inside your home, or some other accident there, but flooding from a storm, or from storm drains around your property—no. You need a special policy. In fact, if you live in a flood-prone area, your lender will require you to purchase this special protection, which runs about $100 for $85,000 worth of coverage each year.

Some private insurance companies offer policies, and the federal government also offers flood coverage that can be obtained through any insurance agent or broker. This is provided through the National Flood Insurance Program, administered by the Federal Emergency Management Agency.

If you want flood coverage, whether required by your lender or not, it is best to sign up when you buy your home. There is a waiting period after an application is taken. You cannot ask to have a flood policy written up as soon as you hear that there is a storm heading your way. For more information about federal flood insurance, you can call the National Flood Insurance Program toll-free at 1-800-638-6620.

HURRICANE COVERAGE

A standard homeowners policy provides coverage for windstorm damage, and under this heading comes harm from hurricanes, tornadoes, cyclones, and hailstorms.

If you feel you live in a particularly dangerous locale for these storms—South Carolina, say, or spots along the Gulf

Coast that have been hit heavily, or along a beach—you can purchase a special windstorm insurance policy through an independent company or a statewide insurance pool. Florida, for one, has such a pool, offering windstorm policies to homeowners in its twenty-four coastal counties.

EARTHQUAKE COVERAGE

Earthquake insurance can be secured, for a high fee and high deductible. This is of particular interest to homebuyers in California, where news from seismologists is broadcast more frequently than folks there find comfortable. You can secure an earthquake policy from your homeowners insurance agent. The company *must* offer earthquake protection to Californians.

MORTGAGE LIFE INSURANCE

This is a policy that provides funds to pay off a mortgage if the principal wage earner dies before the loan is paid. If you are at all concerned about such a possibility, look into purchasing term life insurance instead. Mortgage insurance is more costly, and the money from the insurance must be used to pay off your loan. If you still have insurance questions, you can contact your state insurance department for answers to regional situations. You can also call the Insurance Information Institute, the educational arm of the industry, at its toll-free hotline: 1-800-221-4954. Besides answering questions on the phone, they provide to the public brochures and fliers on any type of insurance.

If You Are Buying a Condo or Co-op

In both of these housing styles there are two policies: one is purchased by the owners association or cooperative board for the entire complex, for which you pay a prorated share of premiums as part of your monthly maintenance fee; the second you purchase yourself as coverage for your own apartment and its possessions. There is a special policy for condominium owners, and renters' insurance coverage for co-op residents.

These individual policies are as important for you as insurance is for the master association to carry for common areas. If there is a problem in your unit, such as damaged carpeting from the ubiquitous burst pipes in the unit upstairs, you will need your own insurance coverage. The condo or co-op's policy cannot help you.

Keeping Track of Your Policy

You cannot afford to pay premiums blindly each year and otherwise forget about homeowners insurance. You ought to check your coverage annually and update it if housing prices rise and the replacement cost of your home goes up. If you have bought a fixer-upper and have done extensive—and expensive—remodeling, or if you have purchased new furnishings, you should also make periodic checks of your insurance package. An inflation guard policy that automatically adjusts your plan each year to cover rises in building costs covers only inflation, so you cannot rely on this for total security.

Get Out That
Videorecorder or Camera

Once you are reasonably settled in your new home—
and please do not wait until the last picture is on the
wall—you really ought to put together an inventory of
your possessions. This is a tedious job, but how can you
file a claim for a lost or stolen item if you cannot describe
it to the police so that you stand a chance of getting it
back? And what about the insurance company's need for
verification and a description in the event of theft or loss?
In order to file a claim you have to present an accurate
description and value so that an insurer can determine how
much you are to be paid for them according to the terms of
your policy.

If you do not want to make a written inventory, take a
videorecorder or camera around the house and photo-
graph everything, reading off brand names and serial
numbers as you are shooting or writing them on the back
of photographs. You will at least have a visual record. This
means taking out the jewelry, laying it on the bed or other
flat surface and on a colorless background, and then
shooting each piece of value.

Many police departments around the country offer
etching equipment that residents of their communities can
borrow at no cost to engrave numbers on their valuable
electronic equipment, appliances, and other possessions,
with the numbers then kept by the homeowner and the
police department. You might want this protection, too.

The best way to compile a record of your possessions is
to purchase a household inventory form at a stationery
store. Then go from room to room, listing valuable goods
and appliances and their serial numbers or other identification. We do not all keep receipts religiously, so it is

unlikely you will have all of them to fall back on when a calamity occurs. Even *they* do not always carry a description of the item or its identification number.

Whether you make a home video or write out a household inventory, the document should be stored away from the house, perhaps in a bank safe-deposit box.

A total insurance protection package includes thorough knowledge by you and your insurance carrier of just what you are protecting. Someday you may be patting yourself on the back for the care you have taken in following all of these recommendations.

Tips to Remember

- To save money on insurance: Shop for the best terms, choose the highest deductible you can afford, and pay premiums annually instead of quarterly or monthly.
- Put together some sort of household inventory, even if it is not the comprehensive one suggested by insurance and law-enforcement agencies.
- Review and update your policy periodically.

TWENTY
The Closing: Saving Money Right to the End

The room is hushed. Greetings and forced chatter have given way to the crackle of papers and the occasional voice of a lawyer directing "sign here" and "just initial that."

The solemn proceedings underway are a house settlement, or closing.

After your mortgage has been approved you will be notified of the date of settlement, when the transfer of title takes place. Procedures vary, but certainly the transfer of property titles can be a confusing business for the average consumer. In 1974, RESPA, the Real Estate Settlement Procedures Act, became law. This act governs most of the steps in the transfer of property and protects the homebuyer with its disclosure requirements. Your real estate agent may offer you a copy of the RESPA booklet after your offer for a home has been accepted, or it may come from the lender with your loan package. If you do not see one, ask for a copy.

Keep in mind that unless *everything* is paid at the closing, the property does not change hands. You cannot earnestly plead, "I'll get that check to you when I get paid on Thursday." As soon as it is possible to do so, your lawyer's secretary should call and tell you what your closing expenses will be. If she does not, by all means call her and ask. She may give you a specific figure and ask you to bring to the closing a cashier's check in that amount, made out to the lawyer. In that the money will be paid out in so many different directions, this is only practical. You pay the lawyer for all the charges, and from your money he or she makes disbursements. It would be wise to keep something in your checking account to bring along, in the unlikely event something else pops up that can be paid by personal check.

Closing costs generally run 4 to 6 percent of the sale price of the home, so this can be a considerable expense. However, if you have bought a home with an assumable loan, you need pay only a few hundred dollars at settlement, another advantage of this type of financing.

Here is what you can expect to pay before you truly own your home. Note that there are often no exact figures listed for some of these charges because they vary so from one part of the country to another. These fees can range from $25 to several hundred dollars. Not all of these charges may be applicable where you live, so do not assume that you will be billed for each service listed.

MORTGAGE-RELATED CHARGES

Loan Origination Fee. This covers processing your mortgage. It might be stated as a percent of the loan, or as a flat fee. (This is one of the fees those assuming a loan do not have to consider.)

Loan Discount, or Points. A one-time charge to "adjust the yield" on the loan, which translates into making it more profitable for the lender. One point is 1 percent of the loan. The buyer can pay points, or sometimes the seller does. Buyers using VA mortgages do not pay discount points, but FHA buyers might.

Appraisal Fee. Mortgage lenders require an appraisal of the homes they mortgage, for their own protection. The fee for this is usually paid by the buyer, but can sometimes be paid by the seller, if both agree. The appraisal charge is sometimes included in the mortgage insurance application fee.

Credit Report Fee. This can also be paid when making a written loan application rather than at the closing. In this case, whether you get the mortgage or not, the charge is nonrefundable.

Lender's Inspection Fee. Here is a charge that is applicable to new-home buyers. Representatives of the lender must make several inspections at various stages of the building process.

Mortgage Insurance Application Fee. This covers the processing costs for applying for private mortgage insurance, if you plan to purchase such coverage. Sometimes it is paid in advance of the closing.

Assumption Fee. Those assuming a loan pay this charge, which covers the processing work involved in the assumption.

ITEMS REQUIRED BY THE LENDER TO BE PAID IN ADVANCE

Interest. Usually buyers must pay this charge at the closing. It is interest on their loan for the period of time between the closing date and the date the first scheduled loan payment is due.

Mortgage Insurance Premium. The initial premium is often paid in advance, at the request of the lender. It can cover several months or a full year.

Hazard Insurance Premium. If it has been determined that your home is in an area calling for some type of hazard insurance (flood protection, for example), the lender will require proof of payment of the first year's insurance premium at the closing.

RESERVE FUNDS TO BE DEPOSITED WITH THE LENDER

Hazard Insurance. Some lenders will require that a certain amount of money toward the next year's premium on hazard insurance be held in reserve. At least try to negotiate payment of interest on your reserve fund.

Mortgage Insurance. Some part of this premium may be placed in a reserve account rather than paid in advance at the closing. Again, try to negotiate for interest paid on it, and on any other deposit.

Taxes. This can be a hefty charge of several hundred dollars. Most lenders require a regular monthly payment to the reserve account in your name for city and/or county property taxes. They may also require that an amount equal to six months' taxes be paid at the closing and held in an escrow account. If you can't avoid this, try to knock down the interest paid on this sum.

Special Assessments. Like the tax escrow account, these monies are held in escrow to make payments due either annually or at intervals throughout the year. The funds can be spent for local improvement assessments such as sewers, traffic lights, and sidewalks, or they can represent neighborhood or homeowners' association dues. If you have a clean credit record, ask the lender if you can pay these fees yourself, directly. He or she might say yes!

CHARGES FOR TITLE SERVICES

Title is your right to own the property in question, and proof of such ownership. There are several fees in connection with the process of gaining title.

Settlement or Closing Fee. This amount goes to the closing agent. Whether you pay it or the seller does can be negotiated before the contract is signed.

Abstract or Title Search, Title Examination, and Title Insurance Binder. The latter is sometimes called a commitment to insure. These are charges made for title search and guarantee services. Who pays for what may be dictated by local custom, or by an agreement negotiated before the signing of the contract.

Document Preparation. There could be a separate charge for final preparation of legal papers. Be sure, however, that you are not paying twice for the same service, such as preparation of the mortgage.

Notary Fee. This is paid to a licensed notary public to authenticate the execution of certain applicable documents.

Attorney's Fees. If an attorney is required by the lender for his or her institution's part in the transfer of title, the fee will appear on the Uniform Settlement Statement. If you have privately hired an attorney to represent you, his or her charge will not necessarily appear. Ask your attorney how it is being handled in your situation. It *is* money due at the closing.

Title Insurance. A lender's policy might be required; a policy for the new homeowner may be offered as an option. The premium for each is a one-time charge. Sellers sometimes pay for an owner's policy as part of the seller's assurance of clear title. Buyers usually must pay the fee for the lender's title policy, but often only the amount of the mortgage, not the purchase price of the house, need be insured. All of this is negotiable.

Government Recording and Transfer Fees. Charges for legally recording the new deed and mortgage are usually paid by the buyer. They are set by state and/or local governments. Local government tax stamps may also be required and they, too, carry a fee.

OTHER SETTLEMENT CHARGES

Survey. This is often required by the lender, and often paid for by the buyer. You might be able to save a little money by updating the previous survey made when the seller bought the property.

Termite Inspection. Sometimes required by the lender or local law or custom, this bill is usually paid to those rendering the service in advance of the closing. Who is ultimately charged can be negotiated by buyer and seller, and the account squared at the closing.

Broker's Commission. If you have made an agreement with a buyer's broker, his or her fee will be due at the closing. One expense you do not have to worry about is the seller's agent's commission. The seller traditionally pays this fee.

Other Fees. As mentioned earlier, there is a good deal of diversity in settlement charges, according to each section of the country and taking into account the various types of properties sold. If you are being presented with a bill for still more fees, ask about them until you are fully satisfied with the response.

Is Anything Tax Deductible Here?

Unfortunately, not much. Your portion of any real estate taxes and interest paid in advance is tax deductible. Points are deductible. Your insurance premium is not. Save your itemized list of expenses paid at the closing to show your tax advisor. Most of the other closing costs are not deductible, but they might be added to your home's purchase price to arrive at its adjusted cost basis, so they do serve some tax purpose later.

Buyers always question whether moving expenses are tax deductible. Some are, but the majority are not. Here, too, your accountant can advise you.

More to Do

Aside from the traditional closing costs there are a few other details to see to prior to closing day, and even that morning.

Utilities. Arrange to have the electric and water meters read the morning of the closing, and then have an account established in your name. Do not wait until the last minute. In fact, in dealing with your local water department you might have to make arrangements several weeks in advance. Follow up to see that both have been done.

Fuel. If the house is heated by oil, have the oil company measure what is left in the tank the day before closing, if that is agreeable to the seller. Sellers usually charge buyers for any sizable amount of remaining oil when title switches hands. Otherwise, make some other arrangement. If gas is the fuel, have the meter read on the day of the closing and an account opened in your name.

Before-Closing Inspection. Do it if you can, on the morning of the closing. Make a list of any problems or questions that can be raised at the closing.

Money. During those busy preclosing days, you will want to be sure to purchase that certified check, and to have some money in your checking account in the event something unexpected turns up at the closing.

Your "House" File. In this folder, which you have presumably been keeping since your offer was accepted, you will have a copy of your loan commitment letter and a copy of the contract to purchase. You will also have your homeowners insurance policy and notice of payment of the initial premium, or whatever is required by your lender. The same with any hazard insurance. Bring the file with you to the closing.

Personal Identification. No doubt you carry this around in your wallet or hand bag, but you may need to show some proof that you are who you say you are, so be sure you have a driver's license, passport, or the like with you.

Your wits. Do not assume that you are now in the hands of the professionals, and you can just sit back at the closing and watch the papers fly. Keep alert. Pros make mistakes. Ask questions when you do not understand something, even if you know the questions are those everyone but you can answer. After all, this is *your* $60,000 or $100,000 or $140,000, no one else's. None of those who assisted you during the buying process will care as much as you do about your money, no matter how nice and devoted they have been over the last few months.

Finally, in 'Closing' . . .

Plan to celebrate! You have earned it. Bring champagne to the closing so that you can toast each other later in your new home, where you will no doubt head immediately after you take title. Or make plans for lunch. If you are buying alone, have a special lunch or dinner with friends. This is your first home and it requires some public rite of passage, even if it is more *your* style to drive right over the the hardware store, purchase a mailbox you like and have your name pasted or painted on it! Do *something* you will remember. You have not only just purchased your first home, but you have also bought that house or condominium or cooperative when you thought the odds were very definitely not in your favor.

But just a second. Your housebuying homework is almost over, but not quite. Do follow up with phone calls in a week or two to your lawyer and/or real estate agent for material you did not receive at the closing. It will take four to six weeks for the lawyer to send you a copy of the recorded deed, but other information should be forthcoming more quickly. If *you* don't see that your "home" file is complete, no one will do it for you.

But then, as a successful homebuyer, you already know how much depends on *you*.

Tips to Remember

- Ask about any aspect of the transaction you do not understand.
- Be sure you understand charges, and are not making duplicate payments for services required.
- Depending on how much leverage you have, and how much help you have already won from the sellers with closing costs, try bargaining still further over specific charges.
- Be sure to bring a checkbook to the closing, with some money available to cover the unexpected.

PART VI
HOW TO TRADE UP

TWENTY-ONE
Selling Your First Home

After living in your new home for some time you will probably, at some point, want to move. Where you had the labels first-time buyer and starter-home shopper affixed to you before, you will now hear yourself pegged as a trade-up buyer. There are some important points to consider when pondering that next house. Having *some* breathing space as far as money is concerned—you at least do not have to sweat coming up with a downpayment—does not mean that *this* househunt will necessarily be a cake walk.

What Moving Up Can Do for You

You will continue building equity in your next home, and perhaps appreciation will grow at a faster clip if you head for a particularly attractive, even expensive, neighborhood. Each move you make should build your estate and, with luck, even bring you closer to what you conceive as your dream house. With some folks, their buying and selling houses has left them better fixed financially at retirement than the results of their work life.

What to Watch Out For

There are always cautions with any purchases, but perhaps there *are* fewer of them this time around. You know, after all, the importance of location. You bought your present home knowing which features in a house appeal to buyers and which are turnoffs. You know how home financing works. So, now what is applicable is a few specific points that apply only to a moving-up house-shopper.

• Do not move too soon after buying that first house. If you have bought a first home that you just know you are only going to hold a few years, be very careful that you keep the house *enough years*.

You should not sell sooner than three years, and four is better. Moving is expensive. Even more expensive than the cash outlays attached to the physical hauling of a household from one point to another are the costs you will pay in the transfer of property.

Three years is considered a reasonable point, where, if you are not making money you are at least not losing several thousand dollars. You hope. By three years you could see a small appreciation in the price of your home, which could, say, reimburse you for closing costs. If you move too soon, you will be *out* money.

Let's take an example. Say you paid $85,000 for your starter home. You spent another $3,500 for closing expenses. In year one the economy is just so-so and your home appreciates in value just 3 percent. Now, you estimate, it could bring you $87,550.

Year two is, well, recessionary. You do not want to attach a figure to what you could get for your house now because that number could be lower than your purchase price. But let's assume your house could now fetch its purchase price of $85,000. If you sold in year two you would probably realize less than what you paid, in that you would have to negotiate with the next buyer, who might wind up getting your home for $84,000. So you are out $1,000, plus the $3,500 you spent in closing costs, and probably a 6-percent commission to a real estate agent. *And* you will need another 4 to 6 percent of purchase price for the closing costs on the next place you buy.

An exception to the "don't move too soon" warning might be if you are in a neighborhood sinking into decline and you want to sell at the highest price you are likely to fetch right now. Another exception would be the unexpected corporate move. But there, thankfully, your company will probably pick up most or all of your expenses. But remember, you should not consider buying if you are still frequently transferred. One more situation might be your having bought originally in a community or neighborhood where house prices have risen so dramatically, and the site is so "hot," that you can take a sizable chunk of profit with you, even allowing for that battery of changing-homes expenses.

• Be prepared for a very confused few months, when you become both a homeseller and a homebuyer. This Janus-like sensation was not, of course, present when you purchased your first home, where you could concentrate exclusively on buying. You will get through it, however, and will then be prepared for future house moves, all of which will now involve buying and selling simultaneously.

• If you are moving because you need more space, and are a bit regretful because you do like your present house and neighborhood, consider adding on the room(s) you need. This is a sensible, perhaps even low-cost, solution to getting the house you want without the costs of moving. Consider it. You will have to look into local zoning laws, of course, to see if you *can* expand your home.

The Corporate Transfer

Most companies offer to buy, at fair market value, the home of their transferred employee or, in some cases, to lend him or her the equity in that house without an interest charge, while they manage the property after the family moves out. Manage usually means maintaining the home and paying mortgage installments, insurance, and taxes until the house is actually sold. Most companies also have a specified period of time during which they will pay living expenses while the family househunts and/or awaits closing.

This is an excellent deal because you will know exactly what equity you have in house 1 as soon as the company finishes its fair-market-value appraisals. And you will know that the cash you need will be available for the closing date of house 2.

What you need to be concerned with here is that the closing date on house 2 stays firm, in that you are dealing with, presumably, long distances and do not want to stay in temporary quarters in your new community any longer than you have to. The easiest properties to buy are vacant houses, which are likely to be available exactly when you need them. Avoid houses where the owner wants to sell his or her home before seeking another one, or where the owner is having a new house built and construction has just begun. Also avoid buying a new house yourself if the house is less than almost complete. A good choice: the home of a transferee, who is as eager to sell and move out as you are to buy and move in.

Managing Finances in a Sell/Buy Situation

The most important logistical problem you are likely to have in selling a house and then buying the next one is timing as it applies to getting your equity from house 1 in order to make the downpayment on house 2. The safest switch, or the best procedure when selling and buying, is to sign a contract to sell before you sign a contract to buy. You are looking at houses to buy while yours is on the market, but you restrain yourself from making any firm commitment.

Of course, once you accept an offer on the house you own, you are in a must-sell position. If there is absolutely nothing you want to buy at this time, you can (a) refuse any offers or (b) accept one, but with a distant closing date of perhaps four to six months. The latter is a gamble, of course, but usually it is a safe bet. Just keep in mind that the buyer of your house can go to court to force a seller to close on his property in accordance with the contract, even if the seller has no place to go.

A few other nail-biting scenarios:

• You have bought a new house, the closing date is two weeks away, and you need the cash from the equity in house 1—and there is no buyer in sight.

• The closing date on the old house is the same as the one on the new house. Everything is set. Then the sellers in your new home inform you they will not be able to move for two more months.

• You have bought before you sold and are carrying two mortgages because you still have no buyer for your old house.

WHAT TO DO, AND NOT DO

Some of the nation's largest real estate firms, and some of the nationwide franchises, guarantee the sale of a house in 90 days, or they will buy it. This is not as good a deal as it sounds. The price at which the real estate firm will buy your property is usually between 10 and 20 percent less than its market value, and you must still pay a real estate commission to the broker, even though she is also the new buyer.

A more practical, and more common, solution is the bridge loan, also known as interim financing or a gap loan. This is a short-term, six-month mortgage, where you can draw out the equity on your old home for the downpayment and closing costs on the new one. Once you have sold house 1, you pay off your original mortgage and the bridge loan with the proceeds. Points and origination fees on interim financing are not uncommon; they make the loans more profitable for the lender.

Some lenders require monthly payments on interim financing; others allow the interest to accrue until the time the borrower repays it. Many different types of lenders write these bridge loans: banks, mortgage brokers, finance companies, even some large real estate firms. Terms are variable, so by all means do some shopping before applying for a loan. Check Fannie Mae, too, for information about their Magnet program, which offers some help by soliciting the employer's assistance.

If you are buying a brand-new development home, your developer is a possible source of help. Many will do anything to assist an interested househunter in buying one of their homes, especially in a slow economy. Because trade-up buyers frequently have the "how do I sell my house in time to buy yours" problem, developers offer a variety of plans to help the would-be buyer do just this.

Many will juggle closing dates to allow you the time to sell your existing home. Some, in very bad times, will even buy the house themselves. Ask, ask, and keep asking for concessions. As you have read in Chapter 11, *everything* in a new house is negotiable, and your asking to be accommodated with a problem unsold home is a challenge the developer has dealt with many times before.

Renting an Unsold House

You might want to rent out house 1 on a month-to-month basis, while continuing to allow real estate agents to show the property. The obvious advantage of this is to have rental income to meet at least part of your mortgage payment. A second advantage is occupancy and maintenance. Even if the furniture is not wildly attractive, a house shows better when furnished than when vacant. You can arrange that the tenant handle the yard work, perhaps with a rent concession. You will not have to worry about vandalism, either, with an occupied house. On the other hand, the tenants could perhaps be uncooperative with real estate agents. They could be untidy, and detract from the look of the house. There could be tax consequences to renting. Give renting careful thought, and by all means talk with your accountant first.

Tips to Remember

- Don't move too soon after buying your present home. You will *lose* money.
- Try not to buy your next home until you have a sales contract on your present home. You do not want to be carrying two mortgages.
- In a corporate transfer, ask for as much help as possible with selling your home.

Glossary

Amortization. Prorated repayment of a debt. Most mortgages are being amortized every month you make a payment to the lender.

Appreciation. The increase in value of real estate due to inflation and other economic factors.

As is. A term used in a contract meaning that a buyer is purchasing what he sees as he sees it. There is no representation as to quality, and no promise of repairs.

Assessed valuation. An evaluation of property by an agency of the government for tax purposes.

Assessment. Tax or other charge levied on property by a taxing authority to pay for improvements such as sidewalks, streets, and sewers.

Assumption of mortgage. Buyer taking over seller's old mortgage, at the interest rate and terms of the original loan.

Buy-down. A temporary reduction in the interest rate on a loan by a lender in exchange for a fee paid in cash at closing. It can lower monthly mortgage payments for two years, generally, and can be paid for by the home seller, a developer, or any other willing party.

Caveat emptor. A Latin phrase meaning "let the buyer beware."

Closing. The meeting of all parties involved in order to transfer title to property.

Closing costs. Expenses over and above the price of a property that must be paid before title is transferred. Also known as settlement costs.

Community association. A group to which one must, or may, join when buying into some developments. Even single-family home communities can form such an association.

Condominium. Housing style where buyers own their apartment units outright, plus an undivided share in the common areas of the community.

Contract. An agreement between two parties. To be valid, a real estate contract must be dated, must be in writing, and must include a description of the property, the place and date of delivery of the deed, and all terms and conditions that were mutually agreed upon. It must also be signed by all parties concerned.

Cooperative. A housing style where buyers purchase shares in the corporation that owns the apartment building. The number of shares varies according to the size of the apartment unit being bought, or its purchase price. Tenant-shareholders have a proprietary lease that gives them the right to their units.

Deed. A written instrument that conveys title to real property.

Default. A breach of contract or failure to meet an obligation. Nonpayment of a mortgage beyond a certain number of payments is considered a default.

Discount. See *Points.*

Downpayment. An initial cash investment in purchasing real estate, usually a percentage of the sale price.

Duplex. A two-family house, or an apartment unit that takes up two floors.

Equity. The value an owner has in a piece of property exclusive of its mortgage and other items. For example, if the market value of a house is $100,000, and the owner has paid off $5,000 of a $75,000 mortgage, the owner has $30,000 equity.

Equity sharing. Style of homebuying where one party puts up downpayment and perhaps closing costs; the other lives in the house and pays the mortgage and other agreed-upon costs.

Both own the property, and agree to sell at a specified date, splitting any profits.

Escrow. Money or documents held by a third party until specific conditions of an agreement or contract are fulfilled.

FHA. Federal Housing Administration, an agency created within HUD that insures mortgages on residential property, with downpayment requirements usually lower than those of the open market.

FmHA. Farmers Home Administration, an agency of the U.S. Department of Agriculture that insures home loans in rural communities at favorable terms to qualified borrowers.

Foreclosure. Legal proceedings instigated by a lender to deprive a person of ownership rights when mortgage payments have not been kept up.

FSBO. (pronounced fizbo). Stands for "for sale by owner," referring to homes being sold without the assistance of a real estate agency.

HUD. U.S. Department of Housing and Urban Development, from which most government housing programs emanate.

Interest. Fee charged for use of money.

Joint tenancy. (with right of survivorship). Property ownership by two or more persons with an undivided interest. If one owner dies, the property automatically passes to the other(s).

Lease/purchase option. Opportunity to buy a piece of property by renting for a specified period, usually one year, with the provision that the property may be bought after or during the leasing period at a predetermined price.

Leverage. The effective use of money to buy property by using the smallest permitted amount of one's own capital and borrowing as much as possible in order to obtain the maximum percentage of return on the original investment.

Lien. A debt on property; a mortgage, back taxes, or other claim.

Loan application fee. Not the same as the loan origination fee, this charge is a stated amount (usually between $50 and $100) you pay to apply for a mortgage loan.

Loan origination fee. An extra charge, paid at the closing, that covers the lender's administrative costs, and often makes the loan more profitable to the lender. It can be either a flat amount, or a percentage of the face amount of the loan.

Manufactured housing. Broadly speaking, homes that are built in a factory, then shipped to the building site where the components are assembled.

Market value. Generally accepted as the highest price that a ready, willing, and able buyer will pay and the lowest price a ready, willing, and able seller will accept for the property in question.

Mortgage. A legal document that creates a lien upon a piece of property.

Mortgagee. The party or institution that lends the money.

Mortgagor. The person or persons that borrow the money, giving a lien on the property as security for the loan.

Multiple Listing Service (MLS). The office that supervises the printing and distribution of listings of properties for sale, shared by members of the local Board of Realtors.

Negative amortization. The practice of *adding* to the principal of a loan when its monthly payments are insufficient to pay the interest due.

Points. Sometimes called discount. A fee that a lending institution charges for granting a mortgage. One point is 1 percent of the face value of the loan.

Prequalifying. Lender's mortgage approval *before* buyer purchases a home.

Principal. The amount of money borrowed; the amount of money still owed.

Private mortgage insurance (PMI). Insurance policy required by most lenders of buyers with low downpayments. Annual premium is a fraction of a percent of the amount of the mortgage.

Real estate broker. A person who has passed a state broker's test and represents others in realty transactions. Anyone having his or her own office must be a broker.

Real estate salesperson. A person who has passed a state examination for this position, and who works under the supervision of a broker.

Real estate taxes. Levies on land and buildings charged to owners by local governing agencies. Sometimes known as property taxes.

Realtor. A real estate broker who is a member of the National Association of Realtors, a professional group. Not every broker is a Realtor (a trademark name owned by this association).

Resolution Trust Corporation (RTC). Government-backed entity that is selling real estate acquired from failed thrift associations.

Secondary mortgage market. Most commonly, the two quasi-governmental agencies, the Federal National Mortgage Corporation (Fannie Mae) and the Federal Home Loan Mortgage Corporation (Freddie Mac), that purchase home loans from lenders and resell to investors, to keep mortgage money flowing to primary lenders.

Settlement costs. See *Closing costs*.

Survey. An exact measurement of the size and boundaries of a piece of land by civil engineers or surveyors.

Tenancy in common. Style of ownership in which two or more persons purchase a property jointly, but with no right of survivorship. They are free to will their share to anyone they choose, a principal difference between this form of ownership and joint tenancy.

Term. The lifespan of a mortgage; usually 15 to 30 years, but any length of time agreed upon by buyer and lender.

Title. Actual ownership; the right of possession and evidence of ownership.

Title insurance. An insurance policy that protects against any losses incurred because of defective title.

Title search. A professional examination of public records to determine the chain of ownership of a particular piece of property and to note any liens, mortgages, encumbrances, or other factors that might affect a title.

Townhome. A two- or three-story city house of some architectural or historical distinction, or a two-story living unit in a complex operating under a shared ownership form of housing.

Trust deed. An instrument used in place of a mortgage in certain states; a third-party trustee, not the lender, holds the title to the property until the loan is paid out or defaulted.

VA loan. U.S. Department of Veterans Affairs-backed mortgage. This federal agency operates a loan guarantee program for honorably discharged veterans, with mortgages calling for no downpayment.

Variance. An exception to a zoning ordinance granted by a zoning official, zoning board, or other official body.

Warranties. Protection plans offered by independent companies, or by developers, against problems with new or resale homes. Coverage can be limited or comprehensive.

Zoning. Procedure that classifies real property for a number of different uses—residential, commercial, industrial, and so on—in accordance with a land-use plan. Ordinances are enforced by a local governing body.